SHATTERED MOTHERHOOD
Surviving the Guilt of a Child's Suicide

Donna F. Johnson

We respectfully acknowledge the wisdom of Aboriginal and Torres Strait Islander peoples and their custodianship of the lands and waterways. The Countries on which Spinifex offices are situated are Djiru, Bunurong and Wurundjeri, Wadawurrung, Gundungarra and Noongar.

First published by Spinifex Press, 2025

Spinifex Press Pty Ltd
PO Box 200, Little River, VIC 3211, Australia
PO Box 105, Mission Beach, QLD 4852, Australia

women@spinifexpress.com.au
www.spinifexpress.com.au

Edited by Pauline Hopkins, Renate Klein and Susan Hawthorne
Indexed by Sherrey Quinn
Cover design by Deb Snibson
Typesetting by Helen Christie, Blue Wren Books
Typeset in Minion Pro
Printed in the USA

ISBN: 9781922964144 (paperback)
ISBN: 9781922964151 (ebook)

A catalogue record for this book is available from the National Library of Australia

This book breaks a very deep silence about mothers whose children have committed suicide. Donna Johnson's voice is a very 'maternal' one: intimate, soft, present, wise, and compassionate. She spent many years working with battered women before she stumbled upon and chose to serve this barely visible group of bereaved mothers. They could not see themselves, or each other, their loss and their guilt were overwhelming. Johnson brought a small group of mothers who'd suffered the same kind of loss together, and they understood each other's pain. In doing so, her work became both politically and psychologically radical.

> —Phyllis Chesler, author of 20 books, among them *Women and Madness* and *Mothers on Trial*, and co-editor/contributor to 60 other books

It's not before time that this much-needed book has arrived. Donna Johnson writes with great compassion about the pain, confusion and guilt experienced by women who have lost a child through suicide. At the same time, she encourages mothers to develop a new consciousness and find the courage to reject the woman-blaming that inevitably comes. Finding such courage is the first step in the journey toward healing.

> —Betty McLellan, Psychotherapist and author of *Beyond Psychoppression: A Feminist Alternative Therapy* and *Truth Abandoned: How Can Democracy Survive?*

In this compassionate, beautifully written book, Donna Johnson provides a space for mothers who lost a child through suicide to be heard and have their bottomless grief and guilt understood. This transformative act of turning women's experiences of shattering pain into the power of story offers a life-affirming gift to both these mothers and the readers.

> —Marjorie Anderson, creative writing teacher and co-editor of *Dropped Threads* with Carol Shields

Donna Johnson's book, *Shattered Motherhood*, takes us to a dark place no mother wants to enter or even contemplate: the suicide of one's child. With her extensive experience leading women's groups, she gently brings us in to what she calls "holy space" with compassion, deep respect for women's grieving, and a sharp feminist analysis of mothering, guilt and atonement. This important book offers solace for mothers, guidance for those supporting women in crisis, and hope for women's liberation, grounded in women talking, alone and together.

—Elizabeth Sheehy, Professor Emerita of Law,
University of Ottawa

As a mother who had her world shattered following the loss of my son to suicide, I highly recommend this wise and wonderful book. Beyond brimming with empathy and understanding, it opened my eyes to how societal expectations of mothers added to my suffering. Mothers drowning in guilt and despair will find a lifeline in this book.

—K. Johnson

Shattered Motherhood is an eye-opener onto the silenced voices of mothers who lost a child to suicide and are socially condemned as the sole culprits by the power politics of motherhood. Johnson overturns the patriarchal construct that coerces women to live haunted by guilt, torture and atonement while men remain blameless, thus extending the eternal narrative of grievous harms done to women in the name of societal norms.

—Omnia Amin, author, translator and Professor in the
College of Humanities and Social Sciences at Zayed University
in Dubai, UAE

Donna's searing prose plumbs the depths of unfathomable loss, revealing the raw reality of a mother losing a child to suicide. With exquisite sensitivity, she captures the bond among women who share grief, guilt, shame, solace, pain, as well as laughter and comradery in their healing journey. Donna unearths the layers of suffering while deftly weaving a narrative that exposes society's role in marginalizing these mothers. This book is an elegy of love, a clarion call for change, demanding recognition and atonement for the patriarchal demonizing and unjust blame placed upon mothers who have endured the ultimate loss.

—Gina Wong, psychologist and professor of perinatal mental health. Recipient of the 2024 Canadian Psychological Association Award for Community Service, Human Rights and Social Justice in Psychology

I love this book so much. Whether by stillbirth, illness or suicide, the loss of a child cuts to the core of mothering like no other loss. In a world where mother-blaming is the norm, many of us internalise this blame and take on the mantle of guilt. I too know that 'maternal guilt is a patriarchal contrivance' but I have seldom seen it explained so well, and the antidote laid out for all to see. For many years I have said to mothers, 'let go of the guilt, it does not serve you'. Donna Johnson says this in her book in so many profound, loving, angry ways which deeply moved me. An exceptionally beautiful must-read for all women, but especially for those of us who mother.

—Janet Fraser, author of *Born Still: A Memoir of Grief*

In *Shattered Motherhood*, Donna Johnson offers a powerful and moving tribute to the suffering of mothers whose children have died by suicide. What's more she provides the essential key to their healing: a community of mothers who have suffered the same loss. Here is a compassionate and compelling roadmap through and beyond mother shame, guilt and despair. Johnson's brilliant and compassionate book centres mothers' unique stories in such a way as to restore their suffering to a new wholeness. A profoundly moving and essential book.

　—Petra Bueskens, author of *Modern Motherhood and Women's Dual Selves*

Donna F. Johnson was born in Montreal, Canada, the youngest of four girls. Her father used to say that he was going to put an ad in the newspaper and exchange his four daughters for one boy. She knew he was joking but also sensed the underlying implication that boys were somehow worth more. Her lifelong passion has been to uncover how the inferior status assigned to females plays out in their everyday lives, particularly in the domain of marriage, motherhood and the family. After graduating with a Masters in Psychology, Donna worked in a battered women's refuge. Along with a handful of frontline workers she helped establish Canada's first monument to women murdered by their intimate partners (1992). She has worked as a crisis counselor in an urban police service; taught feminist social work practice at Carleton University; educated judges on domestic violence; and published countless essays describing the plight of abused women. She is on the Canadian team for Hague Mothers, a global campaign aimed at ending the injustices created by the Hague Convention for mothers and children fleeing abusive men. Donna began writing as a child, composing long letters to relatives in far-flung places. Later she wrote letters to authors reflecting on their work. Invariably they would write back. One of her early letters appears in Alice Walker's 1996 book *The Same River Twice: Honouring the Difficult*.

For mothers who have
lost a child to suicide,
and for all mothers,
in homage, and atonement.

We will feel anguish
and we will feel sorrow
and we will feel uncertainty
and we will feel sadness,
but not guilt, says Agata.

Mariche amends:
We may *feel* guilty but we will
know we are not guilty.
—Miriam Toews, *Women Talking*

Contents

Acknowledgments

Shattered Motherhood arises from an ongoing conversation with mothers, beginning with my own mother and sisters. The joys of motherhood are easy to talk about; the perils and heartbreaks not so much. Thank you to all the women who have confided in me and held sacred space in groups, bravely sharing their stories as mothers who have lost a child to suicide. Thank you for allowing me to accompany you. Special recognition to 'Kate', who has broken the silence about the suicide of a child that occurs in the context of an abusive relationship.

Thank you to my mentors Joan Gawn and Helen Levine for years of non-stop dialogue. An avid reader, Joan Gawn only read books by women, a corrective to the absence of concern for women in books by male authors. She is the only woman I have ever met who highlighted her skills gained as the mother of five children to establish her competency to lead a professional organization.

Helen Levine's valuing of mothers and her analysis of the politics of the family were crucial to my thinking, as was her insistence on 'keeping women at the centre'. Her feminist approach to counselling and social work was truly revolutionary. Helen transformed my practice and my life. I owe her everything.

Jan Andrews and Rose Mary Murphy, my 'local editors' as I came to call them, met with me continually during the writing of this book. I struggle to find adequate words to describe what they gave me. It comes to me in images. A light held when I couldn't see where I was going. A steady hand on the tiller when the winds were strong. Like seasoned shepherds they guarded and guided me, as if my humble book was the only project on earth. Like all great coaches they were enthusiastic, focused, knowledgeable and trusting; helping me to reveal what I know through their belief in what I had to say, and in my ability to say it. It is not too much to say that this book would not have been written without their vision and commitment. Any errors in this book are mine, but any good that comes from it will be a reward rightly shared with them.

Meeting Spinifex publishers Renate Klein and Susan Hawthorne in an elevator in Cardiff was a stroke of fortune. Not only did my book find a home with them, working with Renate and Susan (and their hawk-eyed editor Pauline Hopkins) was joyful and inspiring throughout. As feminist publishers they practice what they preach, committed to life-giving ways of working and 'doing buisness'. I was consistently amazed by the quality of my interactions with them. My correspondence with their recalcitrant, advice-dispensing dog Queen Nala – part-dingo, part-human – was an unexpected gift. Nala's life tips always seemed to come at the right time, and always made me laugh.

Thanks to Canadian writer Heather Menzies, who bothered to send me a note after my very first essay was published. Heather taught me the importance of nurturing the flickering flames of potential in other women. Thank you to all the women who have said to me, "You should write a book."

Thank you to my brother-in-law Brian Hanington for a variety of writing tips and for reminding me, when this book seemed destined to crash halfway through, that the book you start out to write is rarely the book you end up with.

Thanks to the women in my own hayloft: Kate Hughes, Fern Martin, Karen Seabrooke, Simone Thibault, Rose Mary Murphy and Jan Andrews. We have been meeting regularly for 27 years to hold on to our sanity and to envision a world where women matter.

To my partner Gwen: thank you for your philosophical insight and focus on the good. You are as gentle, non-intrusive and light on the earth as I am the opposite. Thank you for always valuing and encouraging my writing. Thank you to partners of writers everywhere, destined to suffer the obsession of the writer without being direct recipients of its rewards.

All feminists build on the work of the women who came before. I am proud to follow in your footsteps.

Ottawa, 27 November 2024

Prologue

This book is written first and foremost for mothers living with the incomparable agony of losing a child to suicide. But it is also a call-to-arms for a society that treats women very badly, perhaps mothers worst of all. Where you find women drowning in guilt, you can be sure patriarchy is lying in ambush.

For the mother of the suicided child, adding to her primal and persistent grief is an unyielding sense of culpability. A mother may spend the rest of her life atoning for her child's suicide. She may not understand how she caused it, but she believes in her heart that she did; suffers as if she did; as if she killed her child with her own hands; responsible by virtue of the fact that she is the mother and by dint of her personal failings as a mother. What she did or didn't do. That she left a troubled marriage, or should have left. That she never should have married in the first place. That she missed the signs of her child's flagging will to live, or didn't take the signs as seriously as she should have. She is the mother and the buck stops with her. She may learn to live with her guilt, make peace with it, but she will probably never get over it.

No one can really understand this suffering but another mother who is living it. She alone knows. This knowing is a lifeline between mothers devastated by child suicide. Knowing is the first theme of this book. I wish to bring mothers who have lost a child to suicide together in the same room for the consolation only they can give to each other. That room will be this book.

The second theme is words. I want to put words on the unique and complex experience of mothers whose kids have taken their own lives.

What happens to us as women matters. That which wounds us matters. We have a right to take up space with our pain and to accurately name it. We have a right – dare I say, a duty – to think about what happens to us, parse its complexities, mine its depths. We have a right to transform shapeless, elusive experience, sometimes preconscious, often buried, into form; into ideas and concepts that we can analyze, claim, refute, reject, build on. We have a right to understand the forces acting on our lives. We have the right to build our own theory. We have a right to envision a different kind of world.

No one much asks women what we think. I do in this book. I invite mothers who have lost a child to suicide to think alongside other mothers floundering in the same perilous seas. To read the words of other mothers, hopefully find aspects of their own experience reflected, and then to find their own words. To join in the process of unravelling and speaking the truths of their own complicated lives. To validate and honour their own pain.

What is this suffering of the mother whose child has taken his or her own life, and which now threatens hers? What is its nature? What are its ingredients, its contours? What is this incredible force known as 'a mother's love'? What is her guilt made of, and why is it as bad in the fifth year and the fifteenth as it was in the first?

I know a mother's suffering is not a simple thing. Much is pure sorrow, the cost of love itself, and duty; the price paid for the extraordinary privilege of bearing and raising a child.

But do we not as a society impose needless suffering on mothers? I think we do, in a myriad of ways. By setting the bar for the 'good mother' impossibly high. By giving her too much responsibility and too little support. By expecting her to be perfect and to have no needs – or dreams – of her own. By saddling her with expectations and presumptions and forcing her to comply or pay a heavy price. By pathologizing her when she breaks down. By trapping her in situations of control, threat and violence.

We make it difficult, often impossible, for women to extricate themselves and their children from unhealthy, even dangerous, situations, rendering them powerless to raise their kids as they would want, in love, peace and security. Justice systems in every country are an abject failure when it comes to protecting women in their role as mothers.

This is the social context in which mothers the world over are consigned to raise their children.

And is the mother not but one influence on her children in an increasingly complex world? Does a mother exist in a vacuum that she alone should shoulder the burden of her child's death? What about the father? The father, for whom the bar for parenting is set absurdly low. The father she perhaps cannot speak the truth about for fear of alienating her remaining children.

The third theme of this book is atonement. Not mothers atoning for their children's deaths, but we as a society atoning to mothers for our grievous failures towards them. I want to turn the concept of atonement on its head and lay the blame where it belongs: at the feet of a society that places little value on women, sets them up to fail as mothers, then gaslights them into seeing their so-called failures as stemming from their personal inadequacies. Patriarchy's coup de grâce is manipulating women into thinking they are responsible for the suicide of their child.

Introduction

> There must be those among whom we can sit down and weep
> and still be counted as warriors. I think you thought there
> was no such place for you, and perhaps there was none then,
> and perhaps there is none now; but we will have to make it,
> we who want an end to suffering, who want to change the
> laws of history, if we are not to give ourselves away.
>
> —Adrienne Rich, *Sources* (1983)

In some respects, I am an unlikely person to be writing about
mothers who have lost a child to suicide, for I am neither a
mother, nor have I ever lost a loved one to suicide.

I became involved in this issue in the mid-2000s when I was
employed in the crisis unit of a Canadian police service. I was
hired primarily for my skills working with battered women –
men's violence in intimate relationships provide the bulk of the
work in any police crisis unit. But we also supported families
through sudden deaths from accidents, homicide and suicide.
We attended a lot of suicides. These deaths are always traumatic,
never more so than when the person who has died is young.
Tragically, suicide is regularly completed by young people of both

sexes, and in my first year with the police I found myself too often sitting down with families where the unimaginable had occurred.

I began to notice a pattern among the survivors. While everyone in the family was profoundly affected by the suicide, the mothers were often paralyzed. While fathers, stepfathers and siblings were usually able to get on with their lives after a time, resuming work, school and social activities, many of the mothers were immobilized. While others in the family felt a measure of guilt, the mothers were often ravaged by shame and self-loathing, viewing themselves as utter failures as mothers. While others in the family felt deep sadness, the mothers often felt a sorrow of such magnitude their very survival was threatened. For the mother, the suicide of her child is a calamity of mammoth proportions. Think of an asteroid slamming into the earth.

No matter how often friends and professionals tell the mother of a suicided child that it is not her fault, no matter how she tries to convince herself of this, she will most likely feel it is very much her fault. Some mothers told me they felt unworthy to walk the earth. Others felt they were going insane; that were it not for their other children they would kill themselves.

One afternoon I was visiting a woman named Judy who was out of her mind following the suicide of her 21-year-old son.[1] To tell you the truth, I wasn't quite sure what to do. I was fairly

---

[1] A note on language. I use terms like 'out of her mind' advisedly. It's an attempt to describe unbearable suffering. It is not meant to suggest a pathological reaction. Historically, women's legitimate reactions to pain, trauma and injustice *have* been pathologized, routinely landing them with psychiatric diagnoses and in mental institutions. (See Phyllis Chesler's *Women and Madness*, 1972/2005.)

new to my role as counselor in the police crisis unit and still finding my way. How do you help people who are suffering to this degree? It's tough to witness, and your impulse is to head for the hills. I knew enough to stay put and just be with her in her pain.

Eventually Judy started to talk. "What kind of mother has a child who commits suicide?" she sneered, the contempt clearly aimed at herself. "What kind of a mother am I that this could happen to my child? That I couldn't see it coming? That I couldn't prevent it?"

I asked Judy if there was anything she could think of that would help. I knew she was already seeing a psychologist. She looked me straight in the eye. "I need to meet another mother who has been through this. I need to see what she looks like. I need to see that she has survived – and that she is not a monster." She was completely self-possessed in that moment.

Her words sent a chill down my spine. Never had a woman given me such profound insight into her inner world with a single word. *Monster.*[2] I knew it was just an expression; that Judy was trying to tell me how guilty and responsible she felt for her son's death. Nonetheless, the term is usually reserved for society's worst offenders. Paul Bernardo, one of Canada's most notorious serial killers, is widely referred to as a monster. I did not know it then, but I know now, Judy was providing powerful insight into the soul-destroying social construction of motherhood; into what we

---

2   "Monster, noun. An inhumanly cruel or wicked person." Synonyms include brute, devil, demon, barbarian, savage, villain and sadist. *New Oxford American Dictionary.*

as a society do to mothers. Her choice of terms was no accident. The problem lay far deeper than her own psychology.

Judy knew intuitively that meeting other mothers in the same boat was key to surviving the guilt, shame and self-loathing that engulfed her. She knew she would only feel completely safe in the company of other mothers whose kids had also taken their own lives. They alone would understand. They alone would not judge her. I don't think she felt deserving of being saved at that point, but like a drowning person, she instinctively reached out a hand.

I combed the community to find a group for Judy. There was nothing. I found groups for survivors of suicide in general. I found groups for parents who have lost a child by any means (accident, illness, drug overdose, etc.). No program had been designed specifically to help mothers explore their complex emotional and intellectual reactions to their child's suicide. Searching provincially and nationally, this seemed to be true across the country. That women might have distinct and incomparable issues and needs following the suicide of their child was not on anybody's radar.

I found this shocking. Given women's primary role as bearers of children; given the unique, profound nature of the mother-child bond; given the high level of responsibility for children foisted on women by society; given all we know about male violence in the family, and the reality that many women are forced to parent, and to grieve, in terrible situations; how is it that the *mother's* experience of her child's suicide has been overlooked as a primary site of care and intervention?

Then again, why was I surprised? Sixteen years working in a battered women's shelter had opened my eyes to how little we care about women, *particularly* in their role as mothers. Any woman who has tried to extricate herself and her children from an abusive man will know what I mean. You'd think it would be 'all systems go' to protect vulnerable mothers and kids. In case after case, I saw women and children hung out to dry by police, judges and child welfare agents, the very people mandated to protect them. I'd had hundreds of conversations with women from all over the world and it was the same everywhere. The laws, policies and practices privilege men. Like it or not, we live in a patriarchy.[3]

What's this got to do with lack of supports for mothers coping with the suicide of a child? I'm describing my own coming to awareness about the general situation women find ourselves in, and ultimately why I did not just hand Judy a pamphlet about existing services and walk out the door. By the time I met Judy, I was highly protective when it came to women. Did I know then that the suicide of a child was a feminist issue? No. It was a new problem for me. But I had seen how patriarchal attitudes and ideas insinuate themselves into society and into women's heads, impacting how we see ourselves and our problems, impacting

---

[3]   "Patriarchy: A system of society or government in which men hold the power and women are largely excluded from it." *New Oxford American Dictionary.*

how others see us, and impacting all our institutions, including the helping professions, of which I was a part.[4]

Mainstream mental health professionals are rarely trained to understand the social context of women's lives. If you don't see the power structure you won't recognize patriarchy's trickle-down effect, and you will miss three-quarters of women's experience. Your work might be okay, but it will never be great, and it might well be damaging. It will certainly never be truly empowering or transformative.

There are no specific supports for mothers whose kids have died by suicide because no one has thought of it. Not out of malice, but from a habit of 'not seeing'. Women may be recognized in our various caregiving roles, or as part of a couple or family, but our status as autonomous human beings is obscured. The idea does not occur that a woman might have her own unique experience of the suicide of her child and her own pressing needs; that this is a loss of a different order of magnitude, fundamentally different from losing a spouse or sibling to suicide, hard as that is, and fundamentally different from the father's. It does not occur that there might be things a mother would not feel free or safe to say in a mixed group, or in a group with her husband, who could well be part of her problem. The distinct situation of the mother is not recognized.

---

4   As an example, abused women frequently report that in couples counseling, the therapist, male or female, aligns with the abuser.

Women need a room of our own, said Virginia Woolf, in order to think freely;[5] in order to explore our lives and thoughts unencumbered. We need these spaces individually if we are to be persons, and we need them collectively if we are to be citizens. We need to come together in small groups to think about our common problems. Much of women's distress is caused by, or exacerbated by, our social conditions, yet we are routinely sent off to psychiatrists for 'assessment' and 'treatment' as if the problem resides in our individual deficits and pathology.

Sarah Polley's film, *Women Talking* (2023), is a dramatic example of what can happen when women come together to grapple with grave circumstances in their lives in an environment where they will not be judged, shamed, blamed or pathologized. The film is based on the novel of the same name by Miriam Toews (2018), which was in turn inspired by events that occurred between 2005–2009 in an isolated Mennonite colony in Bolivia. More than 130 females between the ages of eight and sixty were rendered unconscious by cow tranquilizer and raped while sleeping.[6]

Realizing they were victims of brutal sexual violence by men in their own community, eight women assemble in a dusty hayloft to decide their course of action. There are three options on the table. Do they forgive and forget, as per the requirements of their faith? Do they stay and fight for their rights? Or do they leave?

---

5   Virginia Woolf. (1929). *A Room of One's Own*. London: Hogarth Press.

6   Eight men were convicted. Seven received sentences of 25 years. The man who supplied the animal tranquilizer received 12.5 years. <https://canadian mennonite.org/articles/bolivian-mennonite-rape-trial-ends-convictions>.

A single soul-searching conversation about a particular problem becomes a meditation on the universal plight of women. I was riveted. When the movie ended, I sat in the theatre for the longest time in some sort of exquisite pain. It was agonizing and thrilling at the same time. Eight women had spoken truthfully about their lives for 104 minutes without being interrupted, corrected or told to shut up.

Of course, in reality there was no such empowering process. The women of the Bolivian colony were forced to forgive or face eternal damnation. The elders refused them counseling on the grounds that they were unconscious during the rapes. The community simply moved on. The film is a fable – "an act of female imagination" – allowing us to envision a world where women take power over our own naming and our own lives.

———————

In response to Judy's appeal, I started a group at the police station for mothers whose children had died by suicide. There was no question that it was a matter of life and death for these women, all of whom were trying to survive the first agonizing months after the tragedy. I didn't know much about suicide at that point, but I'd run a great many groups for women. I knew if I could get the mothers in the same room, magic would happen. And it did. The story of that group and what we learned forms Chapter 1 of this book.

In 2009, I spoke about my work with the mothers at a conference in New York City. The conference was wonderfully titled 'Moms Gone Mad: Motherhood and Madness, Oppression and Resistance'. My presentation was published in a book of conference proceedings (Johnson 2012). Eventually I retired from the crisis unit and, away from police work, lost contact with mothers bereaved by child suicide.

When COVID-19 hit and violence against women sky-rocketed in Canada as elsewhere, I decided to lend a hand. I put out a shingle offering online support to women in abusive relationships, adding to my profile that I also run groups for mothers whose kids have died by suicide. I had never stopped thinking about the mothers: the ones I'd worked with, and the ones I didn't know but worried about, hoping against hope that supports had improved. I was tossing a line to see if anyone would grab it.

In the northern spring of 2022, I received an email from a woman whose 29-year-old son had taken his own life five years before. She said she was "still looking for the right kind of support." That connection led to the establishment of a second group. Chapter 2 focuses on that group and the experience of mothers at the five-year point following their child's suicide. Are the questions the same or different for mothers five years down the road? Are the pain and guilt as intense? Does coming together with other mothers help at this stage?

In Chapter 3, I reflect on the particular suffering of mothers who have lost a child to suicide in the context of an abusive relationship.

Chapter 4 takes a deep dive into the politics of motherhood. What does it mean to be a mother in the context of a society that sabotages women who are mothers? Guilt will be considered as a primary mechanism for the control of women.

But what to do? How do women, raised to devalue themselves, forced to deny their own experience or pay a heavy price, muster the psychological resources to survive catastrophic loss? Chapter 5 focuses on women coming together in groups as an essential tool for our empowerment. Feminist consciousness shifts a woman's experience of the world, allowing her to access her own voice and power. In the company of other mothers similarly bereaved, she can begin to take back the goodness and integrity of her relationship with her lost child. She can begin to take back her motherhood.

Chapter 6 provides insights gained from my work in the police crisis unit, offering concrete guidelines for centring and supporting mothers bereaved by child suicide.

In Chapter 7, I call for a paradigm shift. It is not mothers who need to atone for their children's deaths, but men and society that need to atone for the widespread harms to mothers.

Now, let us begin to visualize what might be. The process starts with women talking – in a room of their own.

Chapter 1

The First Year After the Suicide
*You just want to put yourself to sleep for a few
months and maybe you'll get through it*

> I found the pain in the beginning was unbearable. My therapist
> once said to me, 'Your job is to get through the day', and I
> remember thinking, how do I survive the next five minutes?
> —Mary

On 5 February 2007, five mothers who had lost a child to suicide
came together for a series of meetings inside an urban Canadian
police station. It was freezing that day, minus 28°C without the
wind chill. I remember looking out my office window and seeing
Mary walking across the street in her gorgeous winter coat,
steaming coffee in hand. She had managed to arrange time away
from her very senior government post.[7] All the mothers would
make it every week to the meetings for the eight weeks of the pilot
project. And then they would ask for the group to be extended.
And then they would ask for another extension. We ended up

---

7   In 1997, Mary C. McLaren was the first woman to be named Usher of the Black
     Rod, a ceremonial position in the Senate of Canada and the government's most
     senior protocol officer.

meeting for nearly a year. The group became a lifeline that pulled the women though those first excruciating months.

You could be forgiven for thinking it was an odd place for a group of grieving mothers to meet. Police stations are not exactly famous for their coziness, and this one was no exception. The business of justice, catching criminals and all, seems to require ugly concrete walls, harsh lighting and hard furniture. There wasn't a comfortable chair in the building. Try as I might, I could not warm up our meeting space.

The location was chosen because it was where I worked. It was free and convenient. I had been given the green light in my position as a counselor in the crisis unit to run this pilot project for mothers whose kids had taken their own lives. I was trying to keep the costs down and maintain a low profile. My boss had been generous in letting me try this group and I didn't want to push my luck. I needed to be away from my desk as little as possible. A group of this nature was a departure from our normal work supporting people in the immediate aftermath of trauma. A couple of visits after the tragic event and refer on to long-term supports – that was our mandate. But for these women there were no long-term supports. There was nowhere to refer these mothers *to*. No program had been created to help women cope with the life-altering, indeed life-threatening experience of their child's suicide.

In time I would discover a deep irony in the venue. The mothers all felt as guilty as any offender wrestled into the holding cell of a police precinct. All felt responsible for the death of their child. All shouldered the blame very personally. It seemed to me that deep down they all felt like criminals and believed they should be punished.

Most people can empathize to some degree with the pain of losing a child, but few can begin to comprehend the mental anguish of a mother whose child has taken his or her own life. Back then I didn't understand it either. I believe the mothers themselves did not entirely understand what they were going through. Coming together was the first step in really taking hold of their own experiences.

After my boss gave first approval for the formation of the group, we still had to get authorization from on high. Green light given, I set about reviewing the police records and contacting women who had lost a child to suicide in the previous year. Five women agreed to give the group a go. I sat down with them individually to prepare them for our work together. They were all very pleased to have been invited to the group. Maybe 'relieved' is a better word. All were in bad shape. The invitation itself seemed to be a bit of an 'aha moment'. I sensed that, with the exception of Judy, they had not known they needed to be with other mothers until the idea was put before them.

As for me, I was nervous. It had been a while since I had run a group and I had certainly never facilitated one like this. I was no specialist in suicide. I had read as much as I could on the subject, talked to some 'experts', photocopied some handouts, drafted an agenda. It all helped me feel prepared, but I soon learned that as far as the mothers were concerned this wasn't what they needed.

What they needed was to be together. They had read all the same stuff I was reading. It was only helpful to a point, because what they needed had not yet been written. I began to realize as we moved forward that we were breaking new ground.

———————————

At the appointed hour I went to the lobby to collect the women. They had already found each other and were engrossed in conversation. I led them through the security doors to our tiny windowless room, hoping the venue itself – the police station – was not re-traumatizing. All suicides involve police and I did worry that seeing officers in uniform might be triggering. I had prepared tea and provided some little cakes; it was one thing I could do. Later, when I found out that they all liked dogs, I began bringing my four-year-old collie Alice to the group as 'co-facilitator'. You can get away with that kind of thing in a police station because they employ dogs as well as people, so nobody blinks an eye at a dog walking down the hall.[8] The mothers loved Alice and would hang onto her when the going got tough.

What stands out about that first meeting was how instantly comfortable the women were with each other. They embraced each other as if they were long-lost sisters, holding each other wordlessly. I believe the healing began right then and there as they offered each other the compassion and mercy they were unable to extend to themselves.

---

8   Dogs are employed for sniffing, tracking, apprehending – and increasingly, for victim support.

They asked each other about their children first thing, sharing photos of their kids with a kind of reverence. Touching the photos as if in an effort to reach both mother and child; to heal the wound, and in the healing, be healed. To be forgiven. There was a lot of "I know … I know …" From the outset the atmosphere in the room was sacred. That remained true for every meeting. As to my worry about the inhospitable setting, we could have been in a broom closet. It wouldn't have mattered.

If you are a religious person you likely think of God as the source of life. Whatever is the source, perhaps mothers are the closest we get to it; to the sacred; to the mystery of life and creation. Maybe every sorrowing mother is the universe itself sorrowing. I know the love and pain in that room was powerful enough to light up a city.

The women opened up easily, clearly relieved to meet other mothers on the same harrowing journey. Relieved to find their fellow travellers were not monsters at all, but magnificent human beings: thoughtful, intelligent, caring, full of heart and soul. In quiet tones and with gut-wrenching sorrow they took turns talking about their children's lives and deaths.

All the mothers were in their forties and fifties. Two resided in the city, three in small towns. At the time of their child's death all were employed: three with the federal government, one as a teacher, one in a local small business. At the time of their child's death three of the women were married to and living with the child's father. Two had divorced and remarried. All had at least one other child. Three of the mothers described being involved with abusive men and were abused before, after, and even, appallingly, during the suicide crisis. Two of the mothers were still living with their abuser. One was actively trying to leave, the other was more or less resigned to her unhappy situation.[9]

The children, two girls and three boys, were aged 16, 16, 18, 21, and 31 when they died. All took their lives by hanging. Four died in their mother's home; one in the home of his father where he had chosen to live. Three of the mothers were the first person to find their child deceased. One mother was not informed of her child's death straight away and was unable to see him until several days later when he was lying in his coffin.

The sessions were structured with a different topic each week. The conversations were free-wheeling and far-ranging, pivoting according to the mothers' experiences and needs that week. I will use the mothers' own words in an effort to capture the essence of what went on in that room: the intensity and openheartedness as the women struggled with the unbearable gravity of their situation; giving voice to their pain and distress – and torpedoed sense of motherhood.[10]

---

9   The impact of abuse by the husband/father will be explored in detail in Chapter 3.

10   All the mothers' words in this chapter appeared in my original article, 'Creating a Space for Mothers Who Have Lost a Child to Suicide' (Johnson 2012) and are reprinted here with permission.

Most of the mothers described years of distress preceding the suicide. Years of living on the edge with kids who were unhappy and depressed. Trying to get their kids help through doctors, psychiatrists, medication, hospitalization, and sometimes police and courts. They described how they had walked on eggshells, searching for the balance between compassion and tough love. Never feeling they were getting it right.

Nicole explains:

> We were troubled with many issues in our home and I think Brett carried all this pain with him. He turned to drugs to try to escape from the emotional pain. As a mother, I approached many organizations but the help didn't come fast enough. I believe something happened that particular day. Brett felt he couldn't cope and decided this was the best way out.

They described the vacillation between hope and the sickening gut feeling that things were not going to end well. They spoke of ripple effects through the family; of incredible strain on siblings and partners; of never feeling they were parenting adequately.

Several of the kids had made previous suicide attempts. Two of the mothers fully expected their child to complete suicide one day, one was "not surprised," and two were blindsided by the suicide. Those who were to some extent prepared said that in the end nothing could prepare a mother for this level of trauma and tragedy. For a child to take the life their mother has laboured so hard to give and preserve.

The mothers spoke powerfully, often poetically, of the anguish of losing a child and their inability to accept the severing of the mother-child bond. They could not comprehend that they would never see their child again. They simply could not tolerate the proposition, as in, "I'm sorry, this just isn't going to work."[11]

In the immediate aftermath of the suicide, all the mothers experienced a profound disconnection from their own body and from the world. Eleanor[12] describes it this way:

> I felt I was living outside of my body. My body would move around, I would see people, greet them, talk, make the moves, but my mind was elsewhere. I was disconnected. It's a devastation. I continue to ask myself to this day, 'Am I a good mother? How can a mother have two kids with depression? Where did I go wrong?' I revisit it all the time. When I hear comments about 'Oh, my children are involved in sports so they don't get into trouble, my children are doing this and that ...' I feel my inadequacy as a mother. I think there must have been something wrong with me, because it just didn't work out that way.

All the mothers spoke of ongoing, crushing fatigue, describing themselves as barely functioning, hanging on by a thread. They feared that they were not going to make it, yet expressed indifference as to whether they lived or died. They were afraid to show their full grief to family and friends, frightened by their own pain, describing it as a tidal wave that could not be pushed back. They spoke of the pressure, internal and external, to pull themselves together, to pick up their lives and be the person they

---

11   The mothers communicated magnificently even things that did not make rational sense.
12   Eleanor is a pseudonym.

were before the tragedy. This, they said, was impossible. The suicide of their child had changed them, intrinsically, forever.

For some, an inability to function with the normal tasks of everyday life escalated into serious health repercussions. Judy says:

> I started going downhill. Spent my nights walking the house, looking outside for Josh, for his spirit, for his soul. If I saw him I was ready to go with him, because I didn't want him to be alone. Finally, after about three weeks of this, I ended up in the hospital having to be sedated.

Margaret's grief impeded her ability to connect with others, including those who wanted to help her in her stricken state:

> Before William died we all knew, we kind of thought that he might do it, so it wasn't a huge shock … but the devastation! I couldn't eat. I couldn't sleep. In our family no one would talk with each other and you couldn't get comfort from other people. Other people were sometimes afraid to approach you. You felt like you had a hole in your heart and you put one foot in front of the other every day. Just to survive that day was an incredible feat.

The mothers who found their child spoke of the image as permanently etched on their brains. They could not 'unsee' it. On top of the severe shock and trauma of that moment they experienced a surge of feelings that included guilt, denial, detachment and loneliness, as brain and heart grappled with the incomprehensible. Nicole describes the moment this way:

> I found my son when I came back from work, and from that moment I was transformed into a different person. I tried to bring Brett back

to life. I did CPR on him. And I really thought I had brought him back to life! Working on my own child was so overwhelming, on top of finding him. To have that image of finding your son in that state, it's so heart-wrenching, and as a mother that day and the following days I was totally detached emotionally. I felt detached from everyone. I felt alone, I felt angry. I felt the guilt as well.

For Mary, there was something profound about being the one who found her child:

I found Siobhan and I'm glad. First, no one else had to experience it. Second, it's a profound moment of intimacy. There's something quite unusual about that, the fact that you brought them into the world and you are the first one to see them after they've left it. At the same time, it plays to the fact that, yes, I feel totally guilty, so this is what I deserve.

At the other end of the spectrum, being separated from the child at the time of the suicide can bring its own problems. Hard as it is for a mother to see her child in that state, being separated may be harder still. If the suicide happens in another city, or if the mother is – for whatever reason – not immediately notified, she must live with the ongoing pain of having been separated from her child at the time of his or her death.

———————————

The mothers were haunted by images of their child's last moments; by the pain that drove him or her to such a desperate act; by the knowledge that their children died alone, without their mothers. Suicide is by its very nature a lonely, often violent death, the opposite of the 'good death' we would desire for our loved ones. Images of her child's last hours and minutes can torment a mother for years. One mother revealed that, on a night when she was out of her mind thinking about her child's horrifying death, she got a rope, stood on a chair and attached one end of the rope to a ceiling fan. She tied the other end of the rope around her neck and pulled it tight. She was clear that she wasn't suicidal, but wanted to experience what her child went through in her final moments. Perhaps to recreate the moment and be there this time. To symbolically be there, fused with the beloved child, sharing in her suffering. To comfort the child. Perhaps to punish herself for not having being there.

To be able to share such an incident in the group and be fully understood, to not have people overreact, not be carted off to Bedlam was a gift to this mother and to all the mothers.

Then there is the complicated feeling of relief. Relief. A word introduced cautiously, tentatively, only long after trust was established, and even then, only whispered. Dare a mother suggest that she felt relief at the death of her child? All the mothers understood this feeling as part of the unbearable mix of feelings. First one, then another, then another said she had felt it. We spent time exploring relief as an entirely human response to release from ongoing anxiety and distress. The mothers were not relieved at the death of their child. They were relieved at having been delivered from the debilitating fear of the child's death. The fear that every time the phone rang the dreaded news would come.

A recurring theme was the pressure to keep on going, keep on looking after everybody else; to keep it together for the sake of the family. The women were all on the verge of collapse but still comforting everybody else. People who come to the funeral want to speak with the mother. Her other kids are upset. Her husband wants to be intimate; this is his way of getting comfort. Meanwhile the laundry is piling up and the family has to eat. If she is lucky, friends and extended family will step in to help for a time. But each woman spoke of the pressure to get back to her station as quickly as possible. To complicate matters, the suicide of her child has destroyed her trust in herself as a mother, so she may feel the demands to perform her service role even more keenly. What is a good mother, anyway, but the caretaker of the family? Mary laments:

> As mothers you are usually running the house, fixing everything, finding things, making things right. One of the things I found hardest to accept was that I could not change this story. I couldn't make things right. There was nothing I could do. Everything else I could do something about but this was final. I couldn't bring her back.

All the women struggled with their shattered sense of motherhood.

- **Mary:** I still come back to that place fairly often, that yes, if I had been a good mother … My marriage broke up as well before this happened. If that hadn't happened, if I hadn't worked as hard, if I'd been a stay-at-home mom … all those things that might have prevented her …

- **Nicole:** Like all of us I asked, where did I go wrong? What could I have done? Why couldn't I have prevented him from doing this to himself? Regardless of how many people tell me not to feel the guilt, I still do. I still feel guilty.

- **Judy:** I felt like a monster. I thought, oh my God, what am I? What kind of mother am I that this could happen to my child, that I couldn't see this coming, that I couldn't prevent it? There are so many 'what ifs'. And like Nicole said, to go out of the house, it was like I had 'loser' stamped on my forehead. I felt that everybody I walked by was looking at me and saying, 'Oh, *you're* the mother whose child committed suicide.'

- **Margaret:** I lost my sense of motherhood. You blame yourself. What you've done. What you could have done better. After Grant's death I pushed my other children away thinking they don't need me, because obviously I didn't do a very good job.

- **Eleanor:** I feel very little. I'm a teacher and I teach young children. Often in the staff room, people will share comments about parents not being 'good enough' parents … 'Look at the children …' You know, bad parents equals bad children. Very easy equation. Well, how does that make me feel? Not that Claire[13] was a bad child, but what happened to her is certainly not a happy ending. So I am listening to all of this and I'm thinking, can I even make comments? Can I even be part of this group? I feel less than nothing. I just want to disappear. So for the longest time I didn't even go into the staff room. I protected myself. I still feel like an outsider.

- **Judy:** That's how you feel. You feel people are looking at you and judging you. And some people do judge you. Like Eleanor said,

---

13   Claire is a pseudonym.

when you go back to work and see someone coming down the hall and they see you and all of a sudden they make a quick U-turn … It makes you feel so low. I have no self-esteem left. To me being a mother was the biggest joy I had in my life. I loved the fact that I had three boys; that I could rough around with them when they were kids. I couldn't get them into all sorts of sports when I was divorced. But I tried; they got into some stuff. And I question myself on that too, thinking, well, maybe if I had scrounged some more money and gotten them into something else, Josh would be alive now. But you don't know …

- **Mary:** It doesn't matter how many times a professional or someone who is objective tells you that it's not your fault, you can't tell yourself that until … I don't know … I don't know if I'll ever get over that.

———————————

Midway through the pilot we stopped to evaluate how things were going. The women were already worrying about the group ending and brainstorming possibilities to keep it going.

The mothers spoke of the consolation of being in that room. They had found an understanding with each other, a deep knowing they could not find anywhere else. They loved having a few hours in the week where they could focus on themselves, free from their caretaking commitments; free to be themselves, to flounder without fear of judgement or abandonment; free from the pressure to 'get on with it'. Free to search for answers they know they will never find.

In that room they could take up space with their ongoing sorrow, regret, self-doubt, anger. They could go at their own pace.

They could find their own words for their experience. They could say the unsayable.

There was no doubt the group had bonded. I was relieved. But something was bothering me. Nothing could shake the mothers' sense of guilt. Nothing could shake their belief that they were somehow responsible for their children's suicide through their failure as mothers.

Now, I am well aware that guilt is common in survivors of suicide, in fact it is very often the primary emotion. It's completely normal to agonize over whether one's actions or inactions contributed to the suicide of a loved one. But I sensed there was something else going on. There was a different timbre to the women's guilt. Somehow it did not ring true. I recognized that it was sincerely felt. But something was lurking in the shadows.

Their pain I could easily understand. Suicide is a uniquely difficult grief experience, violent and traumatic, surrounded by stigma and shame. And when it's the child you have borne and nurtured, the pain must be near annihilating. I could see that part of the mother had died with her daughter or son that day.

But bad mothers? Feeling they were at fault for their child's death due to their fundamental failures as mothers? I knew instinctively that this was not right; that an unfair, unmerited burden was being imposed on women already suffering to the nth degree.

In my previous work with survivors of battering and rape, I had seen women continually blamed and made to feel there was something wrong with them when they were not at fault at all, and perfectly healthy. I felt an instinctive desire to protect these women from the accusation that they were bad mothers.

The mothers were all the kind of people you'd want for friends. The kind of people you'd want to care for your own children. Notwithstanding their tenacious self-deprecation and persistent trotting out of personal failures, it was not hard to glean from the conversations in the room that they were mothers who loved their children deeply and often went beyond the call of duty to care for and support them. It was they, the mothers, who in the main had shouldered the burden of the deceased child's upbringing and struggles.

And I couldn't help but notice that there was very little talk of the fathers. The fathers seemed to be off the hook in some presumptive way. Those women who had been neglected or abused would speak about it, yet it didn't seem to move the needle on their sense of culpability.

At this point I realized I was in over my head. I did not know how to shift the guilt. And was I even right in wanting to shift it? I reached out for help – and my own deep dive into the politics of motherhood began.

———————

I consulted with Helen Levine,[14] a retired professor in the School of Social Work, Carleton University. Helen had thought,

---

14   Helen Levine, mentor and friend, introduced women's issues and feminist perspectives into the Social Work curriculum in Canada. In 1989, she received the Governor General's Award in Commemoration of the Person's Case for advancing the status of women in this country. She died in 2018, aged 95.

written and taught extensively from a feminist perspective about mothering. Married for more than 60 years ("… to the same guy!" she would add, amusing herself) and with two daughters, Helen had experienced her own painful struggles as wife and mother, struggles which landed her in a psychiatric hospital at around the age of 50. She was insightful about the complexities arising from the suicide of a child, suspecting that the depth of guilt the women were experiencing was directly tied to internalized patriarchal definitions of motherhood, with their impossible prescription for perfection.

Helen listened attentively to my account of what was happening in the group. "You have to help the mothers see that they have been trained to feel guilty," she said. She went to her bookshelves, pulled out a thick, spiral-bound book and handed it to me. It was a monograph she had co-authored while at the School of Social Work: *The Power Politics of Motherhood: A Feminist Critique of Theory and Practice* (Levine and Estable 1981). I'm embarrassed to say my eyes glazed over.

"Helen, what the hell are 'the power politics of motherhood'?"

For me, 'politics' concerned governments, political parties, relations between countries … you know, big stuff, important stuff. Helen and I had talked extensively about all sorts of issues impacting women, but not motherhood. Perhaps because I am neither married nor a mother myself, it had not been a burning question between us. Whatever the reason, it was turning out to be a big gap in my knowledge.

Helen put on the kettle, brought out some store-bought cookies (she hadn't baked for 30 years, since she went on strike in her home and refused to shop, cook or clean any longer), and we settled in. I often took notes when Helen spoke, and I wrote furiously that day as she gave me a crash course on the politics of marriage and the family:

> The picture of *Leave It to Beaver*[15] or whatever is not very real. There are relentless demands and unspoken assumptions embedded in the institution of motherhood, which is in reality a prescription for accommodation, service and perfection. It was Adrienne Rich (1995) who first called it 'the institution of motherhood,' which conveys the idea that there's a prescription for motherhood that all normal women will subscribe to, and if you don't subscribe to it then there is some pathology or there is some distortion, or you need some kind of rehabilitation as a human being.

As Helen poured the tea she began talking about the endless giving and accommodating expected of women. She had a million examples:

> It is simply presumed that the woman will yield her name, mobility, and financial independence in order to become a wife and mother. It is presumed that women will do most of the domestic and emotional work and nurturing of relationships in the family. It is usually mothers who carry the weighty responsibility for child care after separation and divorce. Painful splits and pulls in women's lives are routinely glossed over. 'Motherwork' is the only labour assumed to be undertaken for love and by one sex exclusively. There is no

---

15   A 1950s sitcom based on an idealized view of the family.

training – the work is presumed to be instinctual. Motherworkers sign on indefinitely. There is no sick leave. There are no fixed hours, leaves of absence, vacations or pensions.

It's a recipe for disaster, Helen said:

> Women inevitably become unhappy and angry in the attempt to fulfill this impossible and unfair prescription. It is then that they are often pathologized and medicated, labeled inadequate or unfit; expected to control their feelings and behaviour in the interests of the family. Mothers are expected above all else to maintain the stability of the home, to be a steady source of love and emotional support which needs no refills.

My own mother, who struggled with depression, lived on valium, the drug known as 'mother's little helper'. Pharmaceutical ad campaigns in the 60s and 70s were shamelessly aimed at getting women who were breaking down 'back to their stations'. An advertisement for Serax in the *Journal of the American Medical Association* reads, "You can't set her free. But you can help her feel less anxious" (*JAMA* 1967). Today the drugs are different, the messages more subtle, but when it comes to addressing the underlying conditions of women's lives, little has changed.

Helen went on to explain how guilt, self-blame and low self-esteem are structured into the very heart of women's lives:

> Guilt comes home from the hospital with the baby. Mothers are trained to assume that if anything goes wrong, it must be our own fault. Accordingly, we are constantly assessing our performance in terms of unreachable goals, and apologizing for supposed deficiencies in ourselves and our children. Knowing that others

blame us, we blame ourselves. Is it any wonder that when ultimate disaster strikes in the form of her child's suicide, a mother may find herself paralyzed with the feeling that she is responsible?

I stopped her right there and asked her if she would consider joining the group in the capacity of 'resource person'. It was the smartest thing I ever did. Helen had a genius for explaining our own lives to us as women; a particular gravitas which, combined with humour and a soft voice, gave her a commanding presence. She could sit down in any group of women and begin a dialogue, always starting with herself and her own vulnerabilities, and the space would start to open up, and the coercive forces acting upon our lives would be thrown into relief. Helen could explain patriarchy's trickle-down like nobody else. She made complex feminist theory accessible, perhaps because she came to feminism through the difficult circumstances of her own life. It was not theoretical for her. She often said were it not for feminism she would have lost her mind.

In the sixth week, with the women's permission, Helen Levine came on board. She was 83 years old.

———————

I struggle to express how Helen's coming to the group changed things, because it wasn't linear, and it certainly wasn't hitting the women over the head with theory. It was her self-disclosures about her own mistakes as a mother, and her periods of being lost. It was gentle conversation and encouragement, honouring the mothers for their hard work and devotion to their children.

It was a fragment here, a connection there, an insight, a link. Helen's respect for women, her strength-based approach and her sheer brilliance infused the room with emotional vitality and intellectual vigour.

Women are starved for ideas that accurately describe our lives. Helen helped the mothers take hold of their experience as women and mothers in a world that devalues both. Being a mother can be a valuable and joyful part of life, she said, but the demands and expectations of the role exact a toll. Undervalued, overworked, unsupported, the woman begins to lose herself. When things go haywire in the family, as they inevitably will, it is usually the mother who is held responsible, and who, under these conditions, accepts the blame.

As Helen shared her life and perspective, the women began to reflect on their experiences as mothers in a different way. With the exception of Eleanor's partner, the biological fathers had not been much involved in raising the children. They were largely inaccessible as husbands and fathers due to preoccupation with work, indifference to the domestic sphere, alcohol addiction, or controlling and abusive behaviour.

The women began to consider the huge amount of work and responsibility they had undertaken over the years, parenting with little or no support, sometimes in the face of ill-health and soul-destroying circumstances. They reflected on the sacrifices and accommodations they had made – and the injustices they had endured – for the sake of their children and harmony in the home.

During one meeting, Mary started to weep. She said that she could not figure out what her tears were about. She said she was not a mother who 'gave everything'. She was, after all, a career woman. In fact, had she devoted more of herself to her kids the outcome might have been different.

Margaret said, "I was a stay-at-home mom and look what happened …"

Eleanor stated, "I worked half-time and the end result was the same!"

The women began to laugh, something they had rarely done since their child's death. They had begun to grasp the complexity of their lives and roles; to honour and appreciate all they had tried to give their children. They had begun to feel compassion for themselves; to let themselves off the hook just a little. They had begun to realize, as Canadian suffragist Nellie McClung put it so long ago, that "a bad old lie has been put over on them" (McClung 1915, p. 24). They were not bad mothers at all, but strong and worthy, and good enough, mothers.

At the end of the pilot the women were not ready to say goodbye. They wrote letters to the police service and were granted a brief extension. Helen and I continued to meet with them informally in their own homes for another six months. The group did not change the reality of their child's tragic death. Nevertheless, it did provide a space where each woman could fully process her trauma and loss, and evolve in her understanding of herself as a mother.

As for myself, eventually I retired from police work and lost contact with mothers whose kids have died by suicide. It would be 15 years before I'd work with such mothers again.

I continued to assist women in abusive relationships. My conviction that maternal guilt is a patriarchal contrivance grew with every mother I met.

Chapter 2

Five Years Later

We're expected to be better by now

> The guilt is a burden that magnifies the pain.
> —Kate

It was the COVID-19 pandemic that led, indirectly, to my second round of work with mothers whose children have died by suicide. As more countries went into lockdown we began to hear about a worldwide rising tide of intimate partner violence, an unintended consequence of measures taken to protect public health. For women, isolation is a killer – sometimes literally with the killer in the room.

I decided to 'come out of retirement' to lend a hand. I posted an ad on a counseling website offering online support to women in abusive relationships. It was a big step for me as I am no great fan of virtual communication. Love 'em or hate 'em, these platforms opened up possibilities. As I was about to hit 'send' to submit my profile, I found myself adding that I also run groups for mothers who have lost a child to suicide. I'm not sure what possessed me to put it in; it was more intuitive than anything else. I had never stopped thinking about the mothers; working with them had been among the most powerful experiences of my life. Had supports improved? I think it played on my conscience that I'd let this work slide. Insights from that group had never seen the light of day. The article I'd written was gathering dust in some mouldy archive.

But does caring about an issue qualify you to put yourself forward like this? All the old uncertainties resurfaced. I have no first-hand experience with suicide. I've never borne, let alone lost, a child. I'm not formally trained in this area. Thankfully, at this stage I was able to recognize my insecurities for the imposters they are. "Our doubts are traitors," wrote William Shakespeare, "And make us lose the good we oft might win, By fearing to attempt" (*Measure for Measure*, Act I, Scene IV). I leave it to philosophers to articulate the reciprocal, 'spiritual' relationship between giving and receiving. I knew I had something to give and knew I needed to give it, for the mothers' sake – and for my own. Nonetheless, I remained self-conscious, burying my offering deep in my profile as if hoping no one would contact me.

How do I explain that I can help mothers cope with the suicide of their child based on my experience with domestic violence? I don't even understand it myself. At least I didn't, quite, until I began writing this book. Clearly not all mothers who have lost a child to suicide have been abused by their intimate partner, so that's not the link.

Women's suffering is the link. Thousands of conversations with women have given me insight into the social conditions that give rise to and/or exacerbate women's suffering. These powerful but unseen forces shape women's psychology and determine our behaviour with remarkable consistency. They impact how we think about and manage our distress. They determine how society responds to us when we are distressed. They rob us of our own voice.

I have seen that women's lives are shrouded in silence. What women really think or feel, what really happened, the full story, is rarely articulated. My work has taught me to make space for women's silences: for that which cannot be spoken, lies buried, is not yet known. Women keep silent out of loyalty, out of fear, and from force of habit. I've learned that if women are to reach our full potential, this silence must be broken. Women must lay claim to the power of speech and the power of naming. Harmful and limiting forces acting upon our lives need to be brought out of the shadows. We cannot resist what we cannot see.

I didn't start out knowing this stuff. I learned it by examining my own life and by listening to women. I learned it through sheer repetition of patterns, one story after the other. With a nod to Simone de Beauvoir, one is not born a feminist counselor, but becomes one.[16]

In February 2022, nearly two years after posting my online ad, I received an email from a woman called Kate[17] whose 29-year-

---

16 Feminist counseling is a radical approach to working with women that evolved out of concern that traditional therapies were failing them. See Laura S. Brown's visionary *Subversive Dialogues: Theory in Feminist Therapy*.

17 Kate is a pseudonym.

old son had taken his life five years before. Kate explained that the bereavement groups she had attended had been helpful to a point, but she was "still looking for her people." She wanted to meet with other mothers who had lost a child to suicide.

I responded that I did not have enough mothers to form a group at this time, offering to keep her name and contact her if and when I had the numbers. Wanting to keep the door open and to give her something if I could, I asked Kate if she would be interested in reading an article I'd written about my previous work with mothers who had lost a child to suicide. She said she'd be very interested indeed so I sent it off, along with a note explaining that the piece was 15 years old and may no longer be entirely relevant. I said I'd love her feedback if she felt like giving it.

A few days later Kate wrote back enthusiastically:

> I've read your article through several times now and have to tell you how powerful and comforting I found it. I have read widely in suicide and grief and never come across anything that spoke to me like this. I recognized myself in all of it, including the presence of an abusive ex-husband, my son's father. I loved the article and the women in it and would have loved to be there and experience this with them. Here's hoping there is another opportunity. Mothers need other mothers!

While I wasn't happy to hear she'd had to wait five years to find a piece of writing that spoke directly to her experience, Kate confirmed my fear that mothers still weren't getting the help they needed to cope with a loss of this order and magnitude. I hadn't met her yet, but her words kindled the fire long smouldering in me. It was time to dust off that article and get it into the mainstream. And maybe it was time to get another group going.

———————————

The first step was to find out if I was allowed to republish the article. Dr Gina Wong, editor of the anthology in which it appears, informed me I needed no special permission to republish.[18] Gina had loved the article and was delighted to hear I was picking up work in this area.

The next step was to speak to the women upon whose lives the article was based, to see how they might feel about republishing. It's a very personal piece of writing in which they had not only bared their souls as mothers, but used their real names and their children's real names. I wouldn't take a step without their explicit permission.

Though it had been 15 years since their children had died, by some miracle I still had all their phone numbers. These are not easy calls to make, and I made them with extreme care. Anyone who works with trauma survivors knows their presence, voice, even their name can be deeply triggering even decades after the tragedy. But I was excited to speak with the mothers, eager to know how they were doing all these years later. I wanted to tell them about my dream of starting a new group. Might any of them

———————————

18 Dr Gina Wong is a Registered Psychologist (AB) and Professor in the Faculty of Health Disciplines, Athabasca University, Canada. Dr Wong has contributed to understanding about the institution of motherhood, particularly in the area of maternal guilt, and has been published widely in this field.

want to be involved in some capacity? I was feeling my way as I went.

The five mothers were generous and open in response. All continue to credit the 2007 group with helping them survive their child's suicide. All agreed to having their names and original words used in any future publication.[19] Regarding further involvement, they were mixed. Two had achieved a precarious balance with respect to their child's suicide and were not interested in opening up the wound through any additional participation. I could certainly understand this.

Four of the mothers were open to speaking further with me and I sat down with them individually over coffee. Our conversations were rich and intimate, as if no time had elapsed. Yet fifteen years of vigorous struggle lay between us, summed up in three little words they all used: "It's been hard." Had they come to peace with their child's suicide? Listening to them, it seemed that it was more an uneasy truce. You learn to live with it because you have to. You learn to stop fighting it. But you never accept it.

I picked their brains for lessons learned over the long haul and for any suggestions they might have for women who find themselves newly bereaved by child suicide. Their main advice? Get into a group with other mothers in the same boat.

Judy was keen to be involved in a new group, should there be one. She said she was now ready to use her experience to help other mothers. It would be a way to honour her son.

---

19   One would later change her mind and opt for pseudonyms.

I pondered my conversations with the 'original mothers' for a few days, then summoned the courage to get back in touch with Kate. Don't forget, *she* had approached *me* for counseling. Now I needed her help. The experience and insight of a mother dealing more recently with child suicide would be helpful in determining next steps. I emailed her asking if she'd be willing to sit down with me to talk about her son's death and what precisely she was looking for that she wasn't getting. I explained I would use her guidance to help establish the need for a new group specifically for mothers. It's an unorthodox way of working but it's how I've always worked: figuring out what's needed in concert with other women. Experience told me it would be good for Kate too, even empowering, to be part of such a conversation.[20]

I gave Kate every opportunity to say no. She didn't say no. She said yes, enthusiastically. A few days later we met for coffee. I chose a place where I knew we could speak privately and without interruption. We talked non-stop for more than two hours. Kate was openhearted and trusting with me. I was deeply moved

---

20 Years ago, I ran a group for women who wanted to kill their husbands. It happened that I had met several women in a short space of time who expressed the same desire. Each had experienced prolonged and unabated abuse and had been forsaken by criminal and family courts. I brought these women together in the hope that through listening to each other they would come to understand their anger as a valid human response to entrapment. By accurately naming what's happening, we empower women to decide a course of action from a position of strength. Of course they didn't really want to kill their husbands. They wanted the violence, controls on their liberty, and harms to their children to end. "We may *feel* homicidal but we know we are not killers" (Toews, 2018, p.159).

hearing about her son Theo,[21] his life and who he was as a person; about who he was to her; and about his death. I continually use the word 'sacred' to describe conversations with mothers about the death of their children. It is always, always, holy ground.

Kate was up-front about the abuse she had suffered at the hands of her son's father. She told me that Theo had been deeply impacted by his father's anger and abusiveness. I suspect knowing of my expertise in intimate partner violence made it easier for her to open up about this painful and private experience. In subsequent one-on-one meetings, Kate and I would explore in depth the impact of her ex-husband's abusiveness on her and on her decisions as a mother.[22] But for now, her son's suicide was her focus. She needed to do some more work on this and remained clear that connecting with other mothers was her priority.

Trying to build on the momentum, and as ever proceeding intuitively, I asked Kate if she would consider meeting with Judy (from the first group) and myself to brainstorm possibilities for a new group. She was game – I liked her spirit! – and the three of us sat down over coffee in a hole-in-the-wall café. The two women connected like a pair of war veterans revisiting the battlefield. They asked each other about their deceased child first thing. "Tell me about Theo." "Tell me about Josh." It was wonderful watching them move with each other, each so open and generous in talking about her son and her own pain and struggles. Both women knew

---

21 Theo is a pseudonym.
22 Kate's abusive marriage is discussed in detail in Chapter 3.

how to listen deeply and to share the space. It's exactly this kind of dynamic that makes groups work. Although at very different points in their journey, Kate in the fifth year, Judy in the fifteenth, both were keen to be part of a new group.

Kate knew two other mothers who might want to join us and undertook to contact them. She also offered to host the meetings at her house. As Judy was the 'old pro', we conceived for her the role of 'resource person'.

Following the meeting at the coffee shop, Kate wrote to me excitedly: "I feel our experiences as mothers are unparalleled, and the idea of sharing and supporting, and receiving support in turn with other mothers who have our experience … it's just amazing!"

The women Kate reached out to said yes. Like her, it had been five years since their children, a son and a daughter, had died. The three had met in a bereavement group five years before.

———————————

Kate, Judy and I met again to discuss the thorny question of opening the group to mothers who have lost a child to a drug overdose, whether accidental or as a result of addiction. It wasn't academic. Kate knew several mothers in this situation who might be candidates for our group. I wasn't sure but leaned towards including them. Kate felt it was not a big stretch to consider a drug overdose a type of self-harm, so she too inclined towards inclusion. Judy dissented, though not without guilt. How do you say no to another suffering mother, especially given the dearth of resources for mothers?

Judy felt that while there would be much common ground, there is something fundamentally different at the heart of the struggle for mothers whose children have died by suicide. "We don't have an out," said Judy. "We cannot tell ourselves it was an accident, or unintentional, or an unfortunate consequence of the drug use. We have to reckon with the reality that our own kids wanted to die, chose to die, by suicide."

In the end we deferred to Judy's long years of experience, deciding our group would be open only to mothers whose kids have clearly died by suicide.

————————

I decided I could not run the group without an experienced co-facilitator. I approached Jan Andrews, friend and colleague; we had worked together in the past running groups for abused women. She agreed on the spot. Jan had recently lost a grandniece to a drug overdose, a tragic death that fell into the grey zone just mentioned, so the subject of maternal grief was close to her heart.

Jan and I sat down with Judy to clarify our respective roles. We then met with each of the new participants via Zoom to prepare them for our work together. We took Kate up on her offer to use her house as a meeting place. We were six women and we were ready to go.

————————

Is six an ideal number for a group? It's small. But it's what we had to work with, and it worked. Though the main 'healing', if you will, would happen between the mothers themselves, Judy, Jan and I formed a stalwart 'caring community' that cradled the mothers as they came together each week to grapple with their pain. We had no illusions. They had gotten this far without us, they were strong women, and we were late to the story. But they were still in pain, and the fact that there were three of us to sit down with them week after week to listen, to care, to make space for their ongoing suffering, I think that mattered. I believe we were an important part of their healing, though of course it's difficult to measure such a thing.

———————————

Our first meeting was held on Thursday 1 September 2022. Kate's home turned out to be the perfect venue. No sterile police station this time round. Kate lives in a classy bungalow with a living room conducive to small group intimacy. As the days grew cooler she would light a fire in the stone fireplace that lined one wall. Her little dog Oliver[23] greeted us warmly each week and attended all sessions. Oliver hadn't really done a proper intake, but we let him stay because he was cute. He also provided comic relief. When the women would become upset or sad he seemed to yip or sigh at all the right moments. He did have boundary issues however, and we were forced to closely guard our snacks. Kate had the coffee on every week and always served home baking. It was a beautiful, nurturing space. Never underestimate the importance of taking care of women, so often the ones providing care.

---

23   Oliver is a pseudonym.

We began by establishing ground rules for participation, standard stuff like confidentiality and commitment. We clarified the roles that Jan, Judy and I would play and proposed a structure. We'd meet on Thursday mornings for two and a half hours, for eight weeks. We'd begin each session with a go-around where each woman would have the floor and a chance to talk about her personal situation. We'd break for 20 minutes then have a discussion on an agreed-upon topic. The meeting would end with a quick go-around to make sure everybody was okay.[24] Judy, our beloved resource person, would participate fully in the group, sharing in all the exercises.

For the first meeting we had the mothers introduce their deceased child with photos and stories of his or her life. Each woman described her child's strengths and accomplishments as well as his or her sorrows and struggles. Each described the day or days surrounding the suicide, revisiting events as if they had happened yesterday. Clearly it was all still very fresh. Some were more stoic in the telling; others, more emotional. The mothers who were tearful admired the ones who seemed more together. The mothers who could not cry admired the ones who could. One woman spoke of being crazy with pain at the time of the suicide. Another wondered why she had been so calm during the

---

24 This is a typical structure for a feminist meeting. The facilitators too 'check in' and 'check out'. It's not only a way of equalizing power but demonstrating we are all in this together as women, navigating our lives in a patriarchal world. But the facilitators have a job to do and do not take up space with their problems. Their personal disclosures must be limited and in the interest of moving the process forward.

immediate crisis. She wondered why she had not completely lost her mind.

The women opened up easily to each other, clearly relieved to speak with other mothers who knew exactly what they were going through. Relieved to have a place where they could speak truthfully about how very hard it is even all these years later. Relieved from the burden of having to hold it all together, to be 'better', to be 'over it'. I was immediately struck by how similar their feelings and experiences were to mothers struggling in the first year.

We brainstormed topics for discussion, recording their ideas on a flip chart and referring to the list continually over the eight weeks.

1. Managing the relentless sorrow
2. Guilt, shame
3. Anger
4. The tension between holding it together and allowing ourselves to be a mess and ask for (and get) what we need
5. The expectation on us to 'accept it'; 'be over it'; having to mask the pain so others feel comfortable
6. Taking up space for ourselves as women and as mothers
7. Our experience is not the same as that of the husbands/fathers
8. Impatience with or evil thoughts about people who are continually insensitive
9. Questions that are never going to be answered
10. Regrets
11. Lack of control
12. How to live with all of this and be kind to ourselves

As a result of illness and scheduling conflicts, our eight-week group stretched out over four months. This suited the mothers, who quickly came to dread the group ending. Here in this room, they had permission to be their whole, sorrowing selves. This is not to say they were only sad. There were many laughs in that room, and other kinds of stories told.

———————

I am an inveterate note-taker. As the mothers spoke I would jot down as many notes as I could, trying not to be completely crass but convinced it was important to capture what was happening. I knew it was extraordinary. First, there was the mere fact of 'women talking'; the mere fact of women coming together to grapple with their own lives. Then there was the space itself, the mothers' 'hayloft'[25] – away from the exigencies of their day-to-day lives; out of range of the 'panopticon' of motherhood.[26] The room was at once battleground, neutral zone, sanctuary and shrine. Then there was the subject matter. Sitting down week after week with mothers labouring to come to terms with the suicide of their child, I knew I was witnessing a struggle at the heart of life itself.

In *Women Talking*, the females in the colony can neither read nor write, barred from education by virtue of their sex. Wanting their conversations recorded, they appoint a young teacher by

---

25 In *Women Talking*, the hayloft is the space where the eight women meet.
26 The panopticon is a mid-18th century prison design where cells are placed in a circle around a central station from which the prisoners can be observed twenty-four hours a day. It is a compelling metaphor for society's constant surveillance of mothers.

the name of August Epp to take the minutes of their meetings. The only male who appears in the movie, August is assigned a privileged seat as note-taker/witness-bearer. While the women's act of meeting is risky (they have a small window while the men are away from the colony dealing with the sexual assault charges), their hubris to record their deliberations is truly seditious. They not only assume the right to think for themselves but deem their reflections important enough to record – as if their thoughts mattered.[27]

It occurs to me now that I performed the role of minute-taker in the group – self-appointed in my case – to document the mothers' conversations. It also occurs to me that I have been taking the minutes of women's lives for decades.

I mentioned the flip chart on which we recorded our brainstorming sessions. Sounds pretty tame, the flip chart. You can't get more low-tech, more old-school. Early on in my work at the shelter I saw how women are empowered by seeing their own words captured on the flip chart. We'd fill page after page, then tape the pages to the walls, often filling the whole room with the women's words. They would stand agog, dumbstruck at seeing their thoughts and experiences, routinely trivialized to the point of near extinction, given form through the power of words and a pen.

---

27 Nelly McClung, gifted writer and humorist, penned two razor-sharp chapter titles in her 1915 book of essays, *In Times Like These:* "What do women think of war? (not that it matters)"; and "Should women think?" I recall my own mother often saying to my father, "Clearly, what I think doesn't matter."

My notes for the mothers' group are patchy, and almost illegible at times. As with all minutes they reflect, to an extent, the minute-taker's bias. I am going to write down here – as if on a flip chart – words, themes and questions as captured in my notes. They will be presented as an amalgam. I will collapse themes and alter the record both for concision and to protect privacy. Only Kate will be quoted directly, for she alone consented to have her story told.

Reviewing the minutes, I see the words 'guilt' and 'regret' on nearly every page. The words 'isolation', 'disconnection', and 'loneliness' also appear regularly. The mothers at the five-year mark are still in significant pain. They came to the group precisely because they couldn't live with the pain of their child's suicide. They continue to be plagued by 'what-ifs'. The sense of having failed as mothers continues to have the upper hand. They continue to speak of regrets and to agonize over what they did or failed to do. Five years later, the mothers are still deeply sorrowing. Missing their kids is an ache beating at the centre of their lives, every minute of every day.

If you are a mother who has lost a child to suicide, I hope you will find solace in the honest testimony of this small band of warriors.

"But," you might ask, "the mothers are still suffering terribly, how is this supposed to be comforting?" I turn to my notes to answer this question. At the end of the very first meeting the women are united in this observation:

We are all very different, but we have all ended up in the same place: disconnected, lonely, filled with sorrow, guilt and regret. We are all going through the same thing. In a weird way, this is comforting.

For mothers at the five-year mark, there was massive comfort in knowing they were not alone in their continued suffering:

> We are here because we can't live with it. This is central. Five years later, the 'what ifs' are even stronger, the pain is stronger. But there is less support. People have moved on. We are expected to be okay. We are not. We're expected to be over it. We are not. We second guess our grief, tell ourselves we should be fine by now. And we want to be fine, we want to be out in the world contributing.
>
> We have to distract ourselves. It's a constant struggle between distraction and engagement. We have to do a great deal of pretending. You annoy people when you don't pretend. You have to put on a happy face.

For some of the mums, the grief has changed over time. In the beginning it was more physical. Now it is a softer grief. For others, the pain is still very physical:

- A piece of me is gone. I think of my child morning, noon and night. I feel raw and exposed, as if I have no skin. I'm impatient all the time. That is my main emotion. I'm not a crier, my emotions are not close to the surface, but I think about it all the time. I cannot bear the thought that my child died alone.
- It is as if my child just vanished. My life ended that day.
- How do you find meaning and joy when you have lost your child? It's been five years. Where do I go now? How do I build a life around this hole?

- How are we to reconcile ourselves to the fact that we gave our children life and they chose to end it?
- I have so many regrets. The sorrow, the guilt, the shame are relentless. Our motherhood has been shaken to the core.
- Evil thoughts? I have so many! Every time there is a birthday or celebration I want to hide. I cannot be around small children.
- Platitudes from the medical professionals about suicide prevention just make things worse. 'A comforting hand can make all the difference'. Seriously? How does that make us feel?
- I have a good support system, nevertheless I feel so lonely at times. In the end, we are alone with our grief.
- How do you manage people's insensitivity? How do you manage family relationships? Some people pretend everything is fine; others are clumsy and try to do better next time. Others keep getting it wrong. They never ask about my child or how I am doing.

In the beginning, Jan and I felt it was our job to try and shift the pain, to help the mothers 'feel better', and to this end we introduced various readings, poems, books. Our interventions pretty much flopped. The mothers would listen politely to what we had to say, to our brilliant insights, and after a respectful moment turn back to each other and reengage in lively conversation.

Here's an example. Midway through the group, I travelled to the UK to attend a women's rights conference. Though not religious, when I am in London I like to attend mass at St Martin-in-the-Fields, Trafalgar Square, to hear the music. It happened that on this Sunday, a female priest delivered a brilliant sermon about the plight of people in exile, refugees and so on; people banished from life as they have known it and unable to return. The gist of it was that, faced with unalterable circumstances, you can continue to live as a refugee year after year, hoping to return to your old life, refusing to put down roots, or you can unpack your suitcases and begin to live in the new place. You can "stop the intense period of mourning (your) life of blessing before and let the small mercies of a new life get through the crack in (your) armour" (Hitchiner 2022).

I was struck by the parallel with the mothers' experience: the idea of the mothers as exiles, expelled from their own lives. Upon my return I excitedly shared the sermon with them. They listened politely; I felt the energy drain from the room; and we took the morning break. Had I made them feel judged? Is there an implied message that they aren't doing it right? After the break I asked for feedback. They were decidedly underwhelmed by the sermon.

On another occasion, Jan read an excerpt from *The Gift* by Holocaust survivor Edith Eger, about "the prison of unresolved grief … As long as she stays in guilt she doesn't have to acknowledge that he/she died … As long as she blames herself she doesn't have to acknowledge that he/she chose to die" (Eger 2020, p. 95). That one went over like a lead balloon. The mothers listened politely, then turned back to talking animatedly with each other.

At first I was confused. But after three or four of these bombs, I realized what was happening and found it quite funny, pointing it out to them. "Hey women, you don't need us! We're superfluous to this process! You just want to be with each other!" Everybody laughed but nobody denied it, because it was true, and it was an important insight. The women did not need our input, did not need 'fixing'; in fact, in trying to 'move them along' we were perhaps unwittingly replicating the messages and pressures they were getting from family and friends. Jan and I realized then that our job was simply to create the space so that the mothers could be together. They were doing exactly what they needed to do every time they turned to each other.

At the conference I had attended in the UK, I had heard Rachel Moran from Ireland speak about the profound sorrow carried by women who have been prostituted, and how important it is for these women to come together to support each other.[28] "Grief needs a home," she said.

Maybe that is what Jan and I were doing: creating a home for the mothers' grief to live in.

───────────

According to my notes, in the fourth meeting the women decided they needed to stop beating themselves up. They needed to forgive themselves; stop focusing on the death and on that night or day.

Jan and I asked if anything had shifted for them in the two months since the group began. "Yes!" they shouted in unison. "Being understood."

───────────

<hr>

28   For the best account ever written of the effects of prostitution on women, read Rachel Moran's book, *Paid For: My Journey Through Prostitution* (2015).

Christmas is coming. The women heave a collective sigh. "[Christmas] is a time, of all others, when Want is keenly felt, and Abundance rejoices" (Dickens 1843). All the mothers celebrate, or used to celebrate, Christmas. Now it's pretty much a matter of endurance. They say they feel particularly lonely during the holidays:

> You have to be okay. You look okay. People think you are okay. No one asks. You know you are not doing well so you isolate, but that doesn't work either. You can't admit you are struggling – it's been four years, five years. The world does not understand that our grief continues.
>
> People write in their Christmas letters about their wonderful lives, how well their kids are doing. This one's at university, that one's volunteering abroad, the other is getting married. It's lonely, isolating, alienating. Tiring.

They talk about how grief makes them small, petty. Small, petty, and tired.

Anniversaries are hard, too. The birthday. The death day. The month. The season. Some of the mothers have stopped celebrating their own birthday because it is just a reminder of the call that won't be coming in.

Vacations and holidays with friends give rise to feelings of disconnection. There is a lot of pretending. Pretending makes them feel worse, panicky.

"The world shrinks. Who do you let in?"

———————————

From my notes, Week Five: "The mothers are at war today."

They talk about the ongoing war between their 'strong self' and the part of them that wants to just cave; to capitulate to sorrow and despair. To stop fighting and give in to being a mess:

> I have to choose whether to let grief engulf me or not. I have to make that choice every fucking day. How do I find meaning, purpose, keep going? It's easy to sink.

They talk about the ongoing war in their heads between knowing they were good mothers and knowing they weren't:

- I know I was a good mother. Not perfect. But all I can focus on is everything I did wrong, both as a mother, and in handling the illness. Why didn't I do more? I'm so angry with myself. I think of all my mistakes. I didn't know enough, didn't see how much my child was suffering. How do I ever forgive myself? My child was alone with those feelings. I did not know how to break through that. I didn't have the skills. I let my child down by not preventing the suicide.

- We remember all we did wrong.

- Well, I definitely didn't handle it well. I challenged her.

- I should have been more challenging.

- We have no one to blame but ourselves.

- I blame my ex.

This bombshell is from Kate. She has taken a risk in introducing her ex-partner's abuse into the room. I know what she means because I know the backstory. But it seems the group does not want to go there. I try to open up the question of the role of fathers, to no avail.

"No one is to blame but the person who took his or her own life," someone says.

In the minutes for Week Six I have noted a shift in the room. The atmosphere is a little less emotional, a little more objective.

"Would you have decided to have kids, had you known?"

That's a hard one. It hangs in the air, unanswered.

"Do you think our kids are in a better place now?"

"No. But their pain is over. Our kids got peace. We didn't. Their suffering is over, but now we are carrying their pain. Now we have taken it over."

"Is it fair to say that as mothers we weren't functioning at 100% when we were dealing with our struggling kids?"

"It's true. We were stretched to the limit day to day. What was put on our plate was very, very difficult."

"I don't know. I don't cut myself any slack."

The mothers discuss whether to share their kids' suicide notes with each other. There is no consensus on this, so the subject is quietly dropped.

Some of the mothers are still dealing with their kids' stuff. Their clothes, their rooms. For some, getting rid of everything seems to help. For others, keeping the child's room intact seems to help.

But actually, nothing helps. I remember Mary saying back in the first group, "You keep grasping for straws. Each one holds for about an hour."

———————————

In the seventh meeting we began to wind things down. Jan and I asked the mothers to reflect on what being in this group has meant to them, and to give us feedback on the process:

- For me, this last year has been the hardest. The pain, torture was waking me up at night. I have been on sleeping pills. What we did here in the group was allow ourselves to feel it. I was suppressing all that pain and guilt and it was causing me massive problems. Now, something has shifted. I am letting go of the guilt.

- The group made me delve deeper. I needed to. I feel better, lighter.

- The group allows our grief to live. It is a space to feel it. We need time to invest exclusively in our grief. When I am fully in my grief, I feel integrated.

- It really worked. There's a magic to it. It's the only place I cry. I have been helped by listening to other experiences and perspectives.

- I'm better even though I'm worse and in more pain, if that makes any sense. Why do I feel better? Because here, I cannot avoid it.

- The fifth year was the worst. I've learned in this group to let the pain happen rather than try to get out of it.

- Coming into this group, maybe I was ready to let go of the guilt and pain, to know that letting go of the grief is not letting go of my child. For me, something has definitely shifted. I feel really well. Thinking about my child is not painful, in fact, my heart swells. It has a lot to do with the group, everything to do with the group. I am not so much thinking about the suicide as I am about my child's life. I used to dissociate, pretend; feel like a fraud. Now I'm feeling it, and I'm feeling more integrated.

- Our group made a real difference. There is something about sharing experiences and feeling less alone that has helped me to come to acceptance much faster that I could have imagined. I am less numb; less able to distract myself.

- Words are so important. They help so very much. Putting words on our unthinkable experience has helped to shift things for me.

- I'm a little better while I'm here. Less alone. Less disconnected. Less lonely, isolated. I'm a little worried about the group ending.

In the final session, the women shared personal victories in their individual battles. Giving away a cherished object. Packing up the child's clothes. Packing up the child's room. Any action taken by one of the mothers in the 'letting go' department was received by the others with profound empathy and quiet praise. All recognized the gut-wrenching nature of these decisions, the mountains climbed to get to the few simple words, "I packed up her clothes this week" or "I packed up his room."

There were victories, too, in the social world. Confronting an insensitive friend. Writing off a persistently indifferent one. A small action taken to make Christmas more bearable. Shredding thoughtless letters. An exit strategy for times when being with people becomes unbearable. A code word or bit of sarcasm to help manage impossible situations. Humour worked well to anticipate and dissipate stress.

———————————

Jan and I wanted to give each of the mothers a little gift to mark the end of our work together. We had both been deeply affected by our time with them and I think it was part of our own letting go. We settled on a simple stoneware coffee mug engraved with their child's name. If we had learned anything from the mothers, it was the importance of saying their child's name.

———————————

From the beginning of the group, the idea had been floated that a piece of writing might come out of our work. The women had read and appreciated my original article; some were writers themselves, and all seemed keen to use their hard-won experience to help other mothers. What such a writing project would look like was yet to be determined. Loosely conceived, it would be the book they had searched for but could not find.

With the group ended and the formal part of our work over, we began to talk in earnest about writing. To start the ball rolling, I proposed we brainstorm a list of topics representing the mothers' key points of struggle and insight over the past five years, then gather and record a group discussion on these themes. It was the process I'd used in writing the first article, excerpting the brilliant bits for publication. I teased the mothers that they would have to be profound for the taping, no pressure. But it was actually not much of a joke because they were all quite naturally profound, their words often spilling into the room as pure poetry.

In the end, three of the four mothers decided against being involved in the writing project (which turned out to be this book). They had different reasons for bowing out. For one, it was recognizing she was not comfortable sharing deeply personal experiences in the public domain. Another had achieved a level of peace and did not want to open up the past. The third was uncomfortable having her child's suicide associated with women's issues and abusive relationships.

They informed me individually via email. I wrote back individually, assuring them I understood and respected their decision. And I did. Being part of a book is a very personal decision, and they were under no obligation to participate. But I took their refusals hard, at least at first, until I got my bearings. It seemed to me I had lost their trust. It seemed to me they were enthusiastic until they grasped that I would be examining their experience as mothers through a feminist lens. This was confusing for me, because it was precisely feminist analysis and ways of working that had made the group so successful. At least that is how I saw it.

"Helen would not have had this problem!" I lamented to Jan. I remain convinced that if wise Helen Levine had been in the group, the women would have understood the connection I had failed to make: that the suicide of a child is, like all issues in women's lives, very much a feminist issue. Be that as it may, they had every right to reject that perspective and to have a very different book in mind, one in which their experience as mothers would be related in a more straightforward way, without 'critique', as it were.

After I settled down, I felt discharged to write the book my conscience compelled me to write. In view of everything I've seen I simply could not write another kind of book. But I continue to mull over what happened.

Kate opted to remain with the writing project. My analysis seemed to resonate with her experience.

───────────

It's tricky, introducing feminist politics into a topic as excruciating as the loss of a child to suicide. Women are reluctant at the best of times to examine the social context in which we live, cautious with good reason, for we pay a heavy price for "unveiling the mind," as Nawal El Saadawi put it (Abdallah and Shaker 2018).[29] When a woman has lost a child to suicide, the stakes are exponentially higher. She is hanging on by a thread; how can she be expected to squarely face the problematic conditions in which she has mothered – and now grieves? She needs comfort, not more disruption. For women do become disrupted, often drastically so, as we begin to grasp the coercive forces acting on our lives. As we begin to recognize that we have been groomed from childhood to accept our secondary status and all the injustices that go with it.

And so I ask myself, who am I to disturb a mother's precarious balance after the suicide of her child? Yet how can I stand by while

───────────

29 Nawal el Saadawi (1932–2021) was a medical doctor, psychiatrist, writer and recipient of honorary doctorates. She was Egypt's most renowned feminist.

women are destroyed by the unwarranted, groundless guilt that is a by-product of our subordination?

At the women's refuge where I worked there hung a poster, prominently displayed, containing the following words:

> In education, in marriage, in everything, disappointment is the lot of women. It shall be the business of my life to deepen this disappointment in every woman's heart until she bows down to it no longer.
>
> —Lucy Stone

At that time in 1986, I had no clue who Lucy Stone was but I didn't care; she was a depressing sod. I hated that poster and wanted to rip it down! Why, in a place like this, awash with sorrow, would they want women to feel *worse*? I was just a kid at the time, fresh out of university, still wet behind the ears. I had followed my intuition in going to work there. I had been sexually assaulted twice. I had seen my own mother dwindle away in marriage. I wanted to help women. I couldn't see how making women feel more disappointed would be helpful. I had no idea at that time that there were deep structures operating on women's lives – on every aspect of our lives – and that there was work to be done by each of us that involved facing up to these structures in order that we might resist them.

Lucy Stone, it turns out, was a prominent American suffragette. She was speaking in 1855 at the National Women's Rights Convention in Cincinnati when she was interrupted by a male heckler who asserted that the female speakers were but "a few disappointed women." The text on the poster was excerpted from her impromptu response. In time, Lucy Stone's words would become the guiding principle of my life and work. Consciousness-raising, helping women think critically about their situation regardless of what problem they are dealing with, would be at the centre of my social work practice.

I make no bones about the fact that I am writing this book in an effort to help alleviate the guilt of mothers following the suicide of their child. When a child dies by suicide the contrivance of maternal guilt operates in a way that is particularly cruel. I wish to expose maternal guilt as a nefarious social construct intended to keep women feeling inadequate – and serving a system that is not in our interest.

Chapter 3

How Partner Abuse Affects the Loss

If I had left earlier, maybe my child would be here today

> When something like this happens,
> there is no language.
> —Kate

Not all women who have lost a child to suicide will have been abused by the child's father, but some, possibly many, will have been, and Kate was one. After the group ended, she asked if I would meet with her individually to help her deal with unfinished business from her first marriage. Thus we embarked upon a series of morning meetings in her home. Kate would serve coffee (and, when I got really lucky, banana pancakes with fruit, yogurt and maple syrup) and we'd settle in across from each other in her cozy living room, aka 'the hayloft', with Oliver the dog up on the back of her chair, draped around her neck.[30] Our conversations typically ran two and a half hours. We'd warm up with a casual chat about books, movies and politics, then the work began. Kate

---

30 Kate said Oliver had played a major role in helping her survive the last five years. How much we owe our four-legged friends for their wordless, soulful presence.

proposed 'mining' as our guiding metaphor. We were mining her history for useful material; disposing of hazardous waste. Kate's capacity for thinking and self-reflection and her willingness to be open and vulnerable has allowed me to write this particularly difficult chapter.

This book is not at heart about violence against women; there are plenty of books on that subject. But it is a book about women, and there is no escaping that where there are women there will be men seeking to control them. Not always, of course, but often enough that we should be on the lookout for it; ever alert to the shame that prevents women from opening up about it.[31] The more complicated the situation, the harder it will be to talk about. When an abused woman loses a child to suicide there are so many layers of guilt and self-loathing to plow through it is hard to know where to begin. This chapter is an attempt to bring this complex experience out of the shadows. Kate will be our guide.

But before taking you to our conversation, I want to say a few words about women's complicated relationship to spousal abuse. Though Kate was keenly aware that she had been mistreated over the course of her 20-year marriage, not all women recognize they have been abused. For some, the fact that they were, or are, in an abusive relationship comes as a revelation. This has nothing to do

---

31 Whenever I am working with women, whatever the presenting problem, I make it a point to ask about male violence in their lives, much as a physician will check blood pressure and other vitals as a matter of course, as fundamental indicators of health. Unaddressed male violence is at the root of and exacerbates many problems, messing with women's thinking, syphoning off their energy. If there has never been any abuse, great; no harm done.

with intelligence. Numerous social and psychological mechanisms mitigate against women seeing our own lives clearly. In the abusive relationship, brainwashing techniques are strategically employed to exert control over even the strongest woman, and before she can turn around, she no longer knows who she is.

At the shelter where I worked it was not uncommon to pick up the crisis line to a small voice saying, "I'm really not sure why I'm calling …" And the woman really wouldn't know, because after years of being told she was stupid, worthless, pathetic, etc., she had lost faith in her own judgement.

Our most powerful educational tool in those days was a three-page handout called 'The Eight Types of Abuse', a list categorizing abusive behaviours under eight headings: emotional, physical, sexual, social, financial, environmental, religious, pregnancy and childbirth (Martin and Younger-Lewis 1997).[32] We'd give it to women, along with a yellow marker, asking them to highlight tactics used by their intimate partner. Women would just whiz through that form, calling out "Check!" or "Tick!" as they highlighted all the terrible things that had been done to them.

---

32 The original list was compiled by men attending an Ottawa program for batterers, many of whom had been convicted of partner assault. The men were asked to list behaviours they had employed to control their wives or girlfriends, or make them feel afraid. Abused women often excuse their partners as 'mentally ill', unable to fathom that a sane person could treat their spouse so cruelly. The list confirmed that these guys know exactly what they are doing. It has been modified and expanded over time, more recently including all manner of violations related to technology and the digital world: cyber stalking, surveillance, image-based sexual abuse, etc.

Kicking, punching or slapping her ✓
Spitting on her ✓
Making her think she's crazy or stupid ✓
Destroying her possessions ✓
Driving fast to scare her ✓
Inappropriate expressions of jealousy ✓
Hounding her for sex or unwanted sex acts ✓
Use of pornography ✓
Exploiting women in prostitution ✓
Insulting her body ✓
Controlling the money ✓
Sabotaging her work or studies ✓
Abandoning her during pregnancy or childbirth ✓
Abandoning her in a public place ✓
Throwing her out of the car ✓
Locking her out of the house ✓
Rubbing her face in a plate of food ✓
Threatening to take the children ✓
Monitoring her whereabouts ✓
Stalking her ✓
Choking her ✓
Raging at her ✓
Abusing her in front of the children ✓
Preventing her from leaving ✓
Turning the children against her ✓
Threatening to kill her ✓

…

And on it would go, the women ticking off all these horrors with unbridled enthusiasm. After witnessing this a number of times I realized what was happening. Women loved this exercise because it validated patterns of control and cruelty inflicted but denied.

Both perpetrator and society engage in this denial. The abusive husband claims his wife is making things up to make him look bad; to get a leg up in custody; to get his money; because she's 'mentally ill', a 'vindictive bitch', etc. Police, courts and child protection agents act in lockstep with the abuser, privileging his word over hers; his rights over hers. The community joins in on the pile on, finding excuses for men even when they kill their wives. Women live in this bizarre universe where the cruelties meted out to them are disappeared: the everyday injustices excused as 'just the way life is'; the rapes, beatings and threats disavowed; the femicides not recognized as violence against women at all, but men 'snapping' under the pressure of their lives. To paraphrase feminist legal scholar Catharine A. MacKinnon, if it happened, it's not a big deal, and if it was a big deal, it didn't happen.[33]

Though women would often break down sobbing at the end of the exercise, 'The Eight Types of Abuse' moved them out of the 'crazy zone' and onto terra firma. I was surprised how quickly they came to see their lives clearly. Consciousness was raised in fifteen minutes.

---

33 Catharine MacKinnon (2006, p. 3) writes, "Before atrocities are recognized as such, they are authoritatively regarded as either too extraordinary to be believable or too ordinary to be atrocious."

It was impressed upon me at the time that the obscurantism surrounding intimate partner violence may be its most damaging aspect. Women cannot resist what they cannot see.

———————————

For Kate there were no big surprises. She was painfully conscious of what she had lived through; excruciatingly aware of the impact of the abuse on her children. Theo was a particularly sensitive child who had often been on the receiving end of his father's rage. The question haunting her was this: If she had left before so much damage had been done, would Theo be alive today? Why had she waited so long to leave?

I ask her to take me back to the beginning; to tell me about her marriage.

"There is so much to 'mine," she says. "There is the getting pregnant story. There is the birth story. There is the medical professionals story."

As Kate's narrative unfolds I realize these are traumatic scenes from her marriage that have never been properly resolved – and by resolved I mean atoned for, as if she were a human being, worthy of reparation. Abused women have armloads of these stories. They are often accused of 'dragging up the past', but holding on to such incidents can be legitimate acts of resistance.

Kate had grown up as a 'lost' middle child in a large, happy family. She met Charles in a fourth-year political science class. He was brilliant and charming. They dated for one and a half years before marrying. She discovered she was pregnant on their honeymoon. She was very ill with nausea and Charles was resentful, blaming her for ruining the honeymoon. She swore at him. He was highly offended. "I have been insulted," he said.

Kate loved being pregnant. She felt confident and empowered. But there was tension. Her new husband drank and was moody and unpredictable. She had hoped to give birth naturally, but in the course of a long and difficult labour the doctors recommended a caesarean. She could hear her husband in the hospital corridor being belligerent with the doctors, telling them off: "We won't have this!"

"It was all about him. Charles felt bullied and pushed around by the doctors."

For the first few months after Theo was born, Kate was on a high. Charles immediately insisted they move from their apartment to a house. He was interested in the baby, but there were frequent temper flare-ups coming out of left-field, usually after he'd been drinking:

> Charles had a public image of being a great guy, but in private he was mean. His parenting was punitive, authoritarian. He was hard on Theo. Alcohol was always involved. He'd apologize, but the cycle would continue. I didn't understand it. Didn't understand this mysterious person. He was very threatening. I tried everything. I'd be quiet. I'd yell back. I thought to myself, 'How am I going to make this work?'

One day when Theo was a year old, Charles punched her in the face.

> It came out of nowhere. I was holding Theo in my arms. I was stunned. I didn't tell anyone. I was embarrassed and ashamed.

He began to drink every day. It was escalating. There was a different feel to it. More aggression. More contempt. He had an anger inside that couldn't be contained. The verbal abuse was off the charts. He would call me terrible names.

I ask her about the names. They are the usual. "Cunt. Slut. Bitch. Whore."

He would withhold affection. He'd give me the silent treatment. He would storm off; I wouldn't know where he was or when he'd be back. He led his own life, had numerous affairs. He controlled the money. His sexual demands were exhausting. It became clear that my body was for the purpose of satisfying his sexual addiction. I was extremely lonely.

When Theo was three years old, Kate called the police. Charles was out of control and she became afraid. She thought long and hard before picking up the phone:

I was terrified to make that call. Terrified of the repercussions. They separated us. He's downstairs, yelling. They calmed him down and left after about 20 minutes. A week later I received a brown envelope in the mail, an info packet on domestic abuse. I skimmed it and tossed it out. I remember not wanting it in the house. I didn't understand what was happening or know how to cope with it.

There were lots of good times. Travel. Camping. Skiing. I ask her what percentage was good. She had obviously thought about this as she had the numbers at hand: "10% great; 40% good; 40% on edge, unhappy, worried; 10% very bad."

In the abusive relationship, mistreatment is never the whole story. Hostilities are interspersed with loving acts and promises to change. Many women experience the abuse as a repetitive cycle with three distinct phases: 'tension building', 'blow up', and 'honeymoon'. The honeymoon phase can keep the abuse going for years.[34]

Abused women often describe their partners as 'Jekyll and Hyde'. When they beat themselves up for marrying, or returning to, guys like this, I remind them that women do not marry, nor return to, abusers. They marry, and return to, Dr Jekyll.

———————

They wanted another child. Kate got pregnant again and this time the pregnancy went smoothly. But she was living a double life. Behind closed doors, Charles continued to be bullying and emotionally abusive. And he issued a warning.

"He told me, 'If you leave me, I will take the kids.'"

A mother only has to hear this once. She is now parenting under threat. It will affect her behaviour and decision-making from this day forward.

"I knew he would oppose me if I left. I just managed it. I put up a facade and kept going."

---

34   At the shelter, I started a group for older women in abusive relationships. The participants were between 60 and 80 years old. One had been raped on her honeymoon. She separated from her husband while in the group, after 50+ years of mistreatment. I still remember some of the things those women said: "I have to find out who I am before I die." "The women who have gone before us have taken their pain to the grave."

Kate had a third pregnancy and miscarried. She was devastated:

> We were supposed to go to Europe. I told him, 'I feel empty.' He said, 'I guess you are, you've lost the baby.' He was derisive and blaming, angry that we had to delay the trip. There is so much power in pregnancy and giving birth, in the mysterious bond between mother and child. His lack of empathy was shattering.
>
> I left when Theo was 19 and away at university. My daughter Chloe was 16. I had taken an apartment. For weeks he phoned me, apologizing, pleading. Things changed after I got a lawyer. He became very angry and bullying ('How dare you?') and cut me off. He told the kids, 'If you support your mother you are not supporting me'. That was his MO: 'If you're not with me, you're against me'. He fought me all the way. Our legal battles went on for years and cost me tens of thousands of dollars. He even approached my boss with false allegations against me, in an effort to humiliate me …
>
> I consider ending my marriage to be the bravest thing I have ever done.

———————

I ask Kate, "What is remaining unresolved in your relationship with Charles?"

She responds swiftly, forcefully. Her self-condemnation has been building as she has exposed her abusive marriage to me. I am reminded of Judy all those years ago, filled with self-loathing; calling herself a monster:

> What kind of person puts up with that for 21 years? Why did it take me so long to leave? Was I using the children as an excuse? How

could I have been so clueless, so unprepared for what I was walking into?

Kate sees the battle. My job is to help her see the war.

In the logic of patriarchy, it is the woman who bears responsibility for the devastation wreaked by her intimate partner. Diminished by the abuse, blamed by perpetrator and society, unable to 'fix it', she absorbs the guilt assigned to her. If she is a mother, the impact of the abuse on her children will be her greatest shame.

There is a lot to feel guilty about.

> Children exposed to the sights, sounds and stress of domestic violence are affected at every age and stage of development. They are at greater risk for emotional, behavioural, social and psychological problems. Children can be affected as if they are being directly abused themselves, and the effects can be long lasting.[35]

Even if the abuse was 'only emotional', kids may suffer serious long-term harm from witnessing repeated acts of violence towards their mother. "Living with violence terrorizes children and presents a formidable barrier to women's resources and confidence to meet their children's needs" (Jaffe and Crooks 2005).

---

35 'The impact of domestic violence on children'. <https://www.gov.mb.ca/justice/vs/dvs/impact.html#:~:text=Children exposed to the sights, behavioural, social and psychological problems>. Retrieved 22 February 2024.

I put down my pen.

"Kate, why did you stay? Why didn't you take the kids and leave?"

It's a 'surgical strike', aimed with precision at a specific target. The target is not her, not her decisions, not her failures as a mother, but patriarchy and its stranglehold on women.

She becomes very quiet, stares at the floor. I am prepared to grab her if she starts to sink.

I had visions, nightmares of them walking to his house, dragging their little Mickey Mouse suitcases behind them. They were so small, so innocent, so vulnerable. He was completely out of control. I knew if we separated he would get generous access, if not joint custody. I knew he would be enraged at me for leaving and that he'd take it out on them. I was too scared to leave my children with him, an abusive alcoholic. I could not bear the thought of them being alone with him. I had to stay in the marriage to protect them. I had no choice.

I lean forward in my chair.

You're right, Kate. You had no choice. It is a terrible failure. But it is not *your* failure. It's society's failure, to women; to mothers. You were sitting on a powder keg. You were trapped. There was no way out. You made a sensible decision given the circumstances.

"End the child's exposure to domestic violence," say the experts. "Children need to feel loved and protected in a safe environment.

Talk to someone you trust and consider ending the relationship safely."[36]

This pearl of wisdom is taken from the website of the Manitoba provincial government, Department of Justice, but it could be from any website, anywhere, that deals with men's violence in intimate relationships. Make no mistake, they are talking to the mother, reminding her that *she* is responsible for protecting her children from abusive men. Women are urged to 'make the right choice' so their children will grow up healthy and happy. But in reality, they have little power to protect their kids from men like Charles.

Women aren't stupid. They know better than anyone that staying with an abusive man will have serious repercussions for their kids, and they suffer tremendously with this knowledge. But they face many barriers when leaving, and they know they will be opposed. Warnings, threats and ultimatums abound at the point of separation, forcing the abused mother to decide between undesirable, often terrifying outcomes. He's *probably* not going to kill her. He's *probably* not going to harm the kids. It will *probably* be okay. But she doesn't know, does she?

Threats to harm or to take the children are the primary weapons for bringing a freedom-seeking woman to heel. Debilitated by years of abuse, frightened for the future, she may come to care little for what happens to her. But she is not prepared to gamble with her kids' lives.

---

36 'The Impact of Domestic Violence on Children'. <https://www.gov.mb.ca/justice/ vs/dvs/impact.html>. Retrieved 11 July 2024.

When a man threatens to take children away from their mother, he manifests contempt for the mother and a desire for absolute power over her. For the mother, all bets are now off. She no longer knows what he is capable of. How far is he prepared to go to keep control of her? How best to protect her children? Like a rat in a maze, she scurries to and fro searching for the right path. Does protecting the children mean she stays? Or does it mean she flees? Which is the road with the least risk?

No woman gets out of an abusive relationship without paying a price. If she draws the short straw, the price will be death for her and/or her children.

———————————

But she has the justice system to protect her, you will say. True in theory. In practice, abused women are more likely to be revictimized than assisted by the courts. In practice, men's rights supersede even those of the women they brutalize. Criminal court interventions are weak to non-existent, leaving women sitting ducks in their own homes. In family court men are given carte blanche to avenge so-called wayward wives, their rights as fathers overriding women's rights to live and raise their children in peace and security. To add insult to injury, it is common for the abuser to wrest children away from their mother only to place them in the care of another female in his life, typically his own mother or new girlfriend. Punishing his ex-partner is the goal.

There is a final, fatal aspect to the justice system's cataclysmic failure towards women. Women who pick up a weapon to protect themselves or their children from violent men are arrested without regard to motive, context and power imbalance, the gravity of their plight obscured. Though they act in self-defence, they are prosecuted as criminals, and if they are mothers they will be separated from their children. Few women are prepared to risk these consequences. Caught between a rock and a hard place, many are murdered in their own homes (Johnson 2022).

Toronto physician Elana Fric decided to make a run for it. "Don't worry, he's not going to kill me," she said to her concerned mother.[37] She thinks she can handle it. She wants to separate reasonably, peaceably, to keep things stable for the kids. But Dr Fric had drawn the short straw, and on 30 November 2016, two days after serving her husband with divorce papers, she died as the result of blunt force trauma and strangulation. While their children slept in the next rooms, Elana's Ivy League-educated, neurosurgeon husband attacked her, breaking her neck and ribs and choking her to death. He cut off her hair, stuffed her tiny body into a suitcase, drove 35 kms and chucked the mother of his children off a bridge.[38]

---

37 'Detective who solved murder of Ontario doctor says killer made big mistake trying to hide his crime'. <https://toronto.ctvnews.ca/detective-who-solved-murder-of-ontario-doctor-says-killer-made-big-mistake-trying-to-hide-his-crime-1.5591745>. Retrieved 23 January 2024.
38 'Elana Fric was killed after filing for divorce. How do we make leaving less dangerous?' <https://globalnews.ca/news/5172976/domestic-violence-and-divorce/>. Retrieved 23 January 2024.

Jennifer Kagan, another Toronto doctor, desperately petitioned the courts to protect her four-year-old daughter from her abusive and unstable ex-partner, citing multiple risk factors. The courts were unmoved. On 9 February 2020, Keira was found dead alongside her father at the bottom of a cliff. The Ontario Domestic Violence Review Committee concluded the child was likely murdered by her father as an act of revenge against his ex-wife, and that her death was both predictable and preventable.[39]

As I write, a 29-year-old Manitoba man has been charged with five counts of first-degree murder for the deaths of his 30-year-old common law partner, Amanda Clearwater, their three young children, and a 17-year-old niece. On 11 February 2024, Amanda's body was found in a ditch. The children – Bethany, six, Jayven, four, and Isabella, two months – were pulled dead from a burning car. Amanda's mother told reporters that her daughter was "a damn good mother," instinctively shielding her from judgement and blame.[40]

On 1 February 2024 in Richmond Hill, Ontario, a mother and her five-month-old daughter were murdered by the baby's father.

---

39 'Report finds Ontario child's likely murder was 'predictable and preventable'. <https://lukesplace.ca/report-finds-ontario-childs-likely-murder-was-predictable-and-preventable/>. Retrieved 17 July 2024. Following her daughter's death, Dr Kagan successfully lobbied for Bill C-233, known as Keira's Law, mandating judicial education on violence against women (Jessica Mundie 2023).

40 'Manitoba man charged with 1st-degree murder in deaths of partner, 3 children and partner's relative'. <https://www.cbc.ca/news/canada/manitoba/carman-deaths-shock-manitoba-1.7112473>. Retrieved 12 February 2024.

Rommelia Asuncion and baby Morgyn died of "severe blunt deep stab wounds."[41]

Despite the prevalence and predictability of these murders, they are routinely cast in the media as 'shocking', 'unimaginable', 'unforeseeable'. The police are always said to be 'searching for answers'; always quick to reassure the community that there is 'no risk to public safety'. This is mystification at work. My personal favourite bit of bamboozlement is the reassurance after every femicide that there is 'no risk to public safety'.[42] Meaning there is no maniac with a gun running around shooting people in the streets. The maniacs inside women's homes are not on the radar.

I make it a point to attend where possible the funerals of women and children murdered in acts of femicide. Standing in a lineup of mourners before up to five coffins I have many times overheard people saying, "But why did he have to take *the kids*?" The kids are seen as innocent victims; the mother, not so much. In the comments section beneath a newspaper article about the murders of Amanda Clearwater and her children and niece, someone wrote: "Condolences to the extended family. It's always tragic when children die."

---

41 "'They should be named": Ontario family speaks after mother, baby murdered in home'. <https://globalnews.ca/news/10292667/mother-baby-murdered-richmond-hill-home-identified/>. Retrieved 20 February 2024.

42 In Canada, on average, a woman is murdered by her intimate partner every six days. In the USA it is every two to three days. Globally, a woman or girl is murdered by a person known to her every 11 minutes. *Killings of women and girls by their intimate partner or other family members.* Report by United Nations Office on Drugs and Crime (2021).

After the separation, Chloe went to live with Charles. She was protective of her father, so Kate knows little about what went on in that house. She does know that there was an incident where Charles grabbed Chloe and pushed her up against a wall. Theo, being the protective brother, went with a friend to confront his father. Charles was incensed by Theo standing up to him. He demanded Theo return his house keys and told him he never wanted to see him again.

Apparently some efforts were made at reconciliation between father and son. Kate recalls Theo saying to her sardonically, "We're supposed to forgive Dad again."

Two years later, Theo took his own life. His father did not come to his funeral. Kate says,

> When Theo died, I blamed Charles instantly. But it was my fault for not stopping him. I further failed by not helping Theo understand his father's abuse. Not talking about it had grave consequences. Theo wasn't coping. Had I handled it differently it could have been a different outcome. It is unbearable, thinking of myself not being there for my kids. It's hard to face.

———————————

I ask Kate to tell me what it was like for her living in that house with Charles:

> I felt terrorized. Tortured. I remember cycling home from work not knowing what I would be facing. What's his mood today? He would explode in rage. His rages were actually impressive, if such a thing applies to something so damaging. They were massive explosions of anger and they were unstoppable until he exhausted himself. There

was no talking to him, no appeasing him or reasoning with him. No amount of pleading would have impact. It was just a barrage, a fire hose of anger and name-calling and hatefulness.

He only hit me once, but he could bully me with his physical power just the same, throwing things across the room and just missing me, hitting walls. He would stare at me like he wanted to kill me. Those eyes struck terror. I would hear about women being murdered by their husbands and sometimes I wondered, am I next? Would he kill me? I would lock myself in the bathroom. He punched the bathroom door.

An image flashes through my mind of Reeva Steenkamp cowering behind the bathroom door. In 2013, the 29-year-old South African model and law graduate was murdered by Olympic athlete Oscar Pistorius, shot four times through a locked bathroom door in his Pretoria residence.[43] I wonder where Theo was when his father was screaming and his mother cowering.

I have known Kate for eight months. Only now is the full context in which her son took his life emerging.

———

I tell Kate about Penny Jackson, the 66-year-old UK woman recently jailed for 18 years for killing her abusive husband with a kitchen knife. The case received international attention due to Ms Jackson's forthright confession, captured on police body cameras

---

43   Pistorius was convicted of culpable homicide. He was released on parole on 5 January 2024 after serving half his sentence.

and released to the public (to massive ridicule). "I admit it all," she says:

> I know what I've done and I know why I've done it, and if I haven't done it properly I'm really annoyed. … I stabbed him … because he's an aggressive bully, and nasty. And I've had enough.

She tells police she is prepared to accept the consequences of her actions and hopes her husband rots in hell.[44]

"She should be giving lessons," says Kate, dryly.

That's the spirit, Kate! I think to myself.

It is not that I am cheering the death of Penny Jackson's husband, nor do I think Kate should be cheering it. I do not want to make light of what happened in the Jackson home that night. It is a terrible, tragic outcome on all fronts.

It's that I hear in Kate's words her fighting spirit. She has recognized in Penny Jackson not a heartless killer, but a woman pushed past the limits of her endurance. In her empathy for another woman, Kate will build empathy for herself and for her own situation.

Penny Jackson suffered decades of abuse at the hands of her husband, a former lieutenant colonel in the British army.[45] I have met a thousand Penny Jacksons in my work. I have never

----

44 'Woman stabs husband and tells police "I admit it all" footage shows'. <https://www.theguardian.com/uk-news/2021/oct/19/woman-stabs-husband-tells-police-admit-all-footage-shows-penelope-jackson>.

45 'Penelope Jackson'. <https://www.justiceforwomen.org.uk/penelope-jackson>.

feared one. Most are out of their minds with pain and fear. They are among the most powerless people on the planet, not because they are weak, but because they are thrown to the wolves by the justice systems in every country. Unprotected as victims, they are prosecuted as criminals when they resort to force in order to stop the torture.

There is no 'Stand-your-ground' law for women. The onus is on us to retreat from our homes. But of course, separation from an abusive man is the time of highest risk. There's the rub.

Kate allows herself to contemplate the idea that if she had killed her husband, her son would be alive today. But we don't know. We do know that she would probably be sitting in a federal penitentiary for the rest of her life, separated from her kids in any case. The injustice of this leads to the next chapter of this book, where I will consider the patriarchal context in which women undertake the role of mother.

Chapter 4

Maternal Guilt

What kind of mother am I that
this could happen to my child?

> Motherhood is guilt. Period.
> —Judy

The loss of a child in any circumstances is a trial that pushes a mother to the limits of her endurance. When the death comes by the child's own hand, the mother is in addition *placed on trial,* in her own mind, and by society. She is still a grieving mother, but one made to feel responsible for her child's death through her inadequacy as a mother. The community may not literally haul her before the courts, but she feels the finger pointing in her direction. "*You're* the mother whose child committed suicide." It must be noted that rarely is a father similarly accused, even if he has been little involved with his son or daughter, indeed, especially if he has been little involved; a cruel irony. But women's lives are filled with cruel ironies.

From the very first time I sat down with mothers whose kids died by suicide and saw how much they suffer guilt, I couldn't bear it. I experienced their being 'in the dock', as it were, as a travesty. I knew in my bones the mothers were wrongfully accused, that the charges were unwarranted and unjust. I wanted to take the guilt off them, but nothing I or anyone else said made a difference.

To be clear, the mothers themselves were not looking to escape blame. On the contrary, they were stepping up for their punishment. Their willingness to accept responsibility for their children's deaths I found, on one hand, deeply affecting. There is much to be admired about women's ethic of care and sense of honour.[46]

Admittedly, the picture is complicated. Acute feelings of guilt are common following a suicide. The mothers, like the rest of us, would have screwed up some of the time. Each woman brought her own baggage (past experiences, traumas, limitations) into her mothering. It is normal to have mishandled situations and to have painful regrets. Moral inquiry and soul searching are good things to do. And the mothers weren't asking to be exonerated. So what was my problem? Why couldn't I just leave them to their guilt?

I was suspicious. I had seen women unjustly blamed before, and what I was observing here did not add up. There was a massive gap between all that the women had done and sacrificed for their kids and their persistent sense of failure. Most had been forced

---

46 If I may give another example of women's honour: women routinely set aside their own needs and grievances for what they perceive to be a higher purpose. I saw repeatedly in my work that in order to protect their children, abused women do not speak ill of the father to them, and in fact work to promote the children's relationship with their father. Conversely, I observed a pattern of abusive men disparaging the mother in front of the kids. This is what happens, but as with so much of men's bad behaviour it is subject to a patriarchal reversal, and in courts worldwide women stand accused of parental alienation. I could write a whole book just about this appalling dynamic.

to raise their children under challenging circumstances. Their profound sorrow I understood. But feeling they were responsible for the suicide because of their failure as mothers? No. I couldn't accept that. It was clear to me that the guilt needed to come off. The guilt must be taken off the mother just as you would remove an arrow from a warrior's chest before binding his or her wounds. I wanted to just yank it out, but I know now it's not that simple, because after this arrow there will be another, and another, and another. I know now that the mothers themselves will have to remove the arrow.

But it's not enough for mothers to tell themselves to stop feeling guilty. The forces acting on our lives are strong and continuous, and they will remain susceptible to the next attack. Removing the guilt will require coming to consciousness about the guilt-producing conditions in which women are forced to live and raise their children.[47] I hope to make these conditions clear in this chapter.

When a child dies by suicide, the mother's guilt does not just show up at the funeral. She has been living with it for a very long time. It has been fuelled throughout her life, stoked in a particular way when she became a mother. Her guilt, though now at catastrophic proportions, must be considered in the context of maternal guilt generally, which in turn must be seen in the context of a woman-blaming society. It's rather like unpacking a set of Russian dolls, one guilt nested neatly within the other. When we

---

47   In a similar process, women who do not do the work of consciousness-raising often find themselves going from one abusive relationship to the next.

get to the last tiny doll we realize that finally, the guilt is being a woman.[48]

"Out comes the afterbirth, in comes the guilt," said Moira.

"Guilt comes home from the hospital with the baby," said Helen.

We joke about it, trivialize it as 'mommy guilt', gift women with candles for the bath, or an afternoon at the spa. Guilty mothers fill the offices of psychiatrists where they are encouraged to seek the roots of their anxiety in their individual psychology. Women are advised to let go, do less, be less controlling, less perfectionist, stop comparing themselves to other mothers, practice affirmations, be more 'grateful'. And of course, take prescription drugs if the attendant depression begins to interfere with 'normal functioning'. The mother's guilt is addressed superficially – she is taught to manage it – and the opportunity to think critically about what is really going on is missed. Rare is the therapist who is prepared to facilitate a deep dive into the oppressive structures that give rise to maternal guilt, what Adrienne Rich dubbed 'the institution of motherhood'.

---

48   It is interesting to note that the innermost doll is typically a baby. The Matryoshka dolls are seen to represent women's traditional role and function in society, passed from mother to mother over the generations. A chain of mothers. Mothers chained. Mothers in boxes. Mothers contained.

Sometimes I think not being a mother myself puts me in a better position to recognize what's happening to mothers. (It has certainly given me more time to think.) Having no skin in the game, I cannot be accused of blowing my own horn when I extol mothers' virtues, nor of being self-serving when I point out that they get a raw deal.[49] Not only are mothers overburdened and under-resourced, but they suffer from 'powerless responsibility'. Adrienne Rich writes of

> the invisible violence of the institution of motherhood, the guilt, the powerless responsibility for human lives, the judgements and condemnations, the fear of her own power, the guilt, the guilt, the guilt (Rich 1976, p. 277).

Mothers are given all the work, little of the credit, all of the blame, and no power to make decisions about their children should a single man oppose them. Children may be the primary responsibility of women, but men have ultimate authority over women and children.

I look around me and see mothers run ragged with responsibility. Given all they do, sacrifice and suffer in their maternal role, why are they all feeling guilty? When *I* am giving more than I can give I typically feel angry and resentful, not guilty. Why is motherhood 'guilt, period'? Is there any other labour we would be

---

49 Even prior to the pandemic, women around the world were outperforming men in unpaid domestic and caring work by a ratio of more than three to one. 'Emergency preparedness requires gender-aware responses to reduce burdens of care, violence and economic insecurity on women'. UN Women and UNDP Tracker Report. Press Release 23 June 2022.

comfortable characterizing this way? Who would want to continue working in an environment where they are constantly failing to meet performance targets? No job is worth the surrendering of your self-respect, particularly one that forces you to work in relative isolation, 24/7, with no benefits and no compensation other than the rewards of the job itself. But of course, women can't just 'walk' because they are tethered to their offspring by love and commitment.

Who benefits from mothers feeling eternally lousy about themselves? How does feeling perpetually inadequate impact women's sense of self? How does it impact their store of resources to cope with life's vicissitudes? What happens when a mother *does* actually mess up, or when her child messes up? What happens when her child gets sick, or slips into addiction, or gets into trouble with the law – or dies? If the worse it gets, the more it is her fault, how is a mother expected to survive when disaster strikes?

Spoiler alert: she's not. From everything I've seen, we don't particularly care if the mother survives. We don't really think about mothers at all, outside of their service roles. We put them in charge, give them all the responsibility, and when they go down with the ship we are okay with it. I think mostly we don't even notice that the mother has slipped beneath the surface.

We have seen what happens in a worst-case scenario of her child's suicide. No matter how much a mother has given or how hard she has tried, no matter the obstacles she has faced or how much she has overcome, the mother sees only that she has failed.

She is haunted by every last thing she did wrong; every time she let her anger show; every time she put herself first. Though friends and professionals urge her to let go of guilt as 'a useless emotion' she is unable to, and her inability to relinquish her guilt is one more sign of her inadequacy. She can't even do grief properly. But the truth is she can't get past it, not because of personal weakness, but because the guilt cultivated in her throughout her maternal journey has reached a destructive climax.

———————

I began to be curious about women's relationship to guilt back in my early days at the shelter. It was the women, the ones who fell traumatized and bleeding through our doors, who felt guilty. Their husbands – perpetrators of often terrible crimes – were cocky and righteous, justified and entitled, blaming their wives with cruel abandon. If any man expressed remorse it was usually a ploy. The women carried the blame for the breakup of the family. Guilt made them stay, guilt made them leave, guilt drove them back home. And guilt made them leave again.

The guilt did not stem from personal pathology or weakness, some sort of fragile inner self, but was a response to concrete circumstances. Their partners were strategic and successful in turning children, courts and community against them. The women did not just *feel* blamed. They *were* blamed, and stren-uously, and if they protested the injustice they were blamed again: cast as angry and vindictive. It is an impossible situation to manage psychologically. In a world where they have little power –

and where nothing makes sense – women are forced to do a whole lot of mental gymnastics to survive.

As the years passed and I spoke with more and more women, I saw that we experience guilt in all sorts of contexts where it doesn't make rational sense, indeed, very often after we have been hurt in some way. Women are placed in impossible circumstances and taught to internalize guilt for things they have absolutely no control over and no ability to change. Gradually I began to see women's guilt as 'the canary in the coal mine', a sign that conditions are toxic and that we may be in trouble if we proceed without taking adequate protective measures.

But what is the danger? What are these toxic conditions acting on women's lives? I am talking about patriarchy, the context of male domination in which we all live. A fuller definition of patriarchy deepens our comprehension. Gerda Lerner, eminent scholar of women's history, traced the roots of patriarchy back to the second millennium BCE. She offers this:

> Patriarchy … means the manifestation and institutionalization of male dominance over women and children in the family and the extension of male dominance over women in society in general. It implies that men hold power in all the important institutions of society and that women are deprived of access to such power. It does not imply that women are either totally powerless or totally deprived of rights, influence, and resources (Lerner 1986, p. xi).

Lerner found that the system of patriarchy can only function if women cooperate with it:

> This cooperation is secured by a variety of means: gender indoctrin-
> ation; educational deprivation; the denial to women of knowledge
> of their history; the dividing of women, one from the other;
> by defining 'respectability' (Lerner 1986, p. xi).

I would add to the list: fear, force, coercive control, and romantic love.

The bad news is that women are complicit in our own oppression. The good news is we can refuse to cooperate. Step one is
seeing the situation for what it is, for we can't change what we
cannot see. We need to become knowledgeable about the systems
and structures that sustain women's inequality. This knowledge
will lead to a sense of our own agency and power to effect change.

But patriarchy is a formidable opponent; a slippery, shape-
shifting monster. Like a pernicious cancer, attacked in one area
it surfaces in another. It excels at subterfuge: mystifying, denying
and reversing reality. Through patriarchal contrivance it is the
woman who is blamed. It is always *her* behaviour, *her* character,
her mental health that are called into question, simultaneously
ensuring that *his* character and behaviour evade scrutiny.

I regard maternal guilt as a uniquely cruel contrivance, mixed
up as it is with the joy of being a mother. It robs women from
the get-go of the full beauty and brilliance of their reproductive
powers. Women feel guilty as they try to avoid becoming

pregnant; if they cannot get pregnant; if anything goes wrong with the pregnancy; if anything goes wrong with the birth; if they can't breast-feed or don't want to; if the baby has problems; if the circumstances in which they become mothers are less than ideal … And this is just the beginning. No mother knows what's in store for her on the maternal journey. But there will be landmines all along the route.

Guilt is the primary mechanism by which women are made to feel responsible for everything that goes wrong in the family. The mother is conned into believing that the problem lies with her and that she can change the situation through willpower and therapy. But the seeds of guilt are planted early and deeply in the life of every female, and once guilt takes hold it becomes very difficult to dislodge. No stick will be needed to make her conform to the requirements of the job, for she has learned to monitor her own behaviour.

I look at the young women around me and see guilt tarnishing their experience of being new mothers. Perversely, guilt leads them to more giving. Mixed in with the responsibilities of being a good mother are the duties of being a good wife, and connected to that is the fear of abandonment. The exhausted mother, tied down with a couple of kids, often financially dependent, conscious of her vulnerability, is afraid to make too many demands on her partner and sets aside her own needs and frustrations in the interest of harmony. More giving builds resentment, which must be repressed because it feels like resentment towards the family, a dangerous, intolerable emotion. But it is actually the institution of motherhood that is causing her resentment.

———————

A South African mother of two writes that the guilt began even before her kids were born. The first father walked out on her during pregnancy. She threw the second one out when she was seven months pregnant.

> I wrote my second year final exams when (my daughter) was a week old, can you imagine the guilt when I had to leave her to go to college! She developed colic on her first month, and as my room was on the sixteenth floor, I visualized tossing her down to the ground below from my window when I was desperate for sleep. I am still consumed with guilt for that.

Forced to rely on her mother and sister for childcare while she works in neighbouring Zimbabwe, she describes herself as collapsing with guilt. "I may need hospitalization soon for the guilt," she writes.[50]

I read about Chinese migrant mothers forced to choose between providing financial support to their children and being physically present to them. The impact on these mothers' self-esteem is enormous. They evaluate themselves very poorly as mothers and in old age try to atone for their absence by taking care of their grandchildren, the children of the children they 'failed' (Li 2002, pp. 1607–1624).

---

50 'Motherhood is a guilty profession'. <https://www.news24.com/news24/motherhood-is-a-guilty-profession-20140717>. Retrieved 13 August 2024.

A Pakistani friend tells me about consoling *her* friend who is overwhelmed with the guilt of being a bad mother. The friend's daughters are at university and doing very well, but they are refusing to wear the veil. Her husband is furious, blaming his wife for his children's 'lack of morals'. My friend tells me that in their culture when a child does well the father receives the credit. When a child does badly or is seen to be doing badly, it is the mother who is blamed and shamed.

I write to my Egyptian friend, Professor Omnia Amin, literary translator for Nawal el Saadawi, inquiring about Nawal's views on motherhood. Nawal was the mother of two children and a keen observer of women's lives. Did she write about motherhood? Here is Omnia's reply:

> Nawal saw motherhood as a prison. She said it imprisons the emotions and the person till they die. I am not sure if you want to incorporate this. But she meant it in terms of liberating the self from the need to be false or to restrict the self for the sake of others who might prevent your growth.[51]

Maternal guilt is universal, it seems. But Omnia cautions me. She knows this is tricky terrain, and that Nawal's words will raise hackles.

---

51   Omnia Amin. Personal communication. 15 February 2023. See Nawal el Saadawi (2017) 'Marriage and Motherhood: A divine double moral code'. <https://sister-hood.com/nawal-el-saadawi/marriage-and-motherhood/>.

Do women really grasp that we live in a patriarchy? I know I didn't, for the longest time. I knew I had to serve men and be wary of them, I knew there was a double standard through and through, but I didn't know there was a name for it.[52] The mothers of the world should be having 'the talk' with their daughters, but most seem to have acquiesced to their subordinate status. While life for females varies country to country, the underlying structure is stable and consistent. We may be forcibly confined to the conditions assigned to us, or free to move about and caught off-guard by the conditions. That's what happened to me. I came face to face with my subordinate status on a speeding train in India, and on a ship in a storm in the middle of the Ionian Sea.

Bear with me as I unpack the Matryoshka dolls. I believe clarity will come for women in a process that begins with honestly examining our own lives. I'll tell you about the events that raised my consciousness, but you will have your own experiences to think about. It's all connected and it's all important. Every single incident is important and needs to be named and recognized as part of the pattern. For women, guilt falls away to the extent that we are conscious.

———————

When I was a student, my mother tried to discourage my friend and I from a one-year travel adventure to India. "The world is not

---

52 Like so many girls I was a 'tomboy', envying boys their privileges, freedoms and more interesting toys, games and sports. A tomboy is an energetic or self-assured girl. The very definition aligns with indices of health.

safe for two women travelling alone," she said. "It's a man's world, Donna, you might as well get used to it." I was strong, assertive and mouthy and figured I could handle myself. And for the most part I did. My friend and I stuck together, and if any guys tried to pull anything we'd tell them we were heading to Calcutta to volunteer with Mother Teresa in her home for dying destitutes (which was true.) They'd always back off. We never knew if it was the death thing that bothered them, or whether they feared being struck down if they interfered with two Catholic girls on a pilgrimage to India. Our clever ruses notwithstanding, I was sexually assaulted twice on that trip. It could have been worse, but back home my mother was lighting candles to the Infant Jesus of Prague for our protection.

There had been numerous incidents prior to this trip, in the streets, on public transportation, in a movie theatre: the minor harassments all young women learn to live with. Pornography was left on my desk in the library stacks, and sent to me at home in a hand-addressed envelope. But the sexual assaults took it to another level, for I experienced myself as 'prey'. They also removed any notion that strength or smarts will protect me. Both men attacked when I was compromised and unable to fight back.

In the first incident I was sound asleep on an overnight train to the south of India. My friend and I were especially cautious at night, but on this occasion the train was packed and there was only space for one of us in the women's compartment. I offered it to her and chose a bunk right outside the door. At dawn I awoke to a sense that something wasn't right. I opened my eyes to the golden light of the Kerala sunrise. A man was sitting on the end of my berth, molesting me. I kicked at him and he slithered off into the bowels of the train. No words were exchanged and I never saw his face. I immediately complained to the conductor, who just smiled and shrugged. I took his shrug to mean, so what do you expect? This is how it is! Please return to your seat.[53]

The incident on the ship also occurred at night.[54] We were travelling between Italy and Greece when a storm blew up and I became very seasick. My friend had a stomach of iron and remained fast asleep in her reclining chair. I went outside to be sick, but half the passengers were out there and I couldn't get a spot at the railing. I staggered back inside and down a staircase in search of a toilet. The silence below deck stays with me to this day. There wasn't a soul around, save for a man in a uniform standing by the bathroom. He opened the door for me. I hurtled past him and threw myself into a stall. He followed me into the bathroom and into the stall and molested me while I was on my hands and knees vomiting. I fought him off as best I could in that position. By the time I was able to stand up he was gone. I never saw his face.

These 'strikes', as I call them, would change the course of my life. I recognized that I was assaulted because I was a woman; a female body, nothing more or less. I was a woman, I was out and about, and that made me fair game. What kind of world was this?

---

53 I've worked with countless women who have been attacked while sleeping. No one believes them.

54 Night is a dangerous time for women, with around 75% of stranger rape occurring between 6 p.m. and 6 a.m. (Lundrigan et al 2022).

In the world I inhabited, people looked out for each other when they were sick, vulnerable or sleeping. To this day I never enter a public washroom without being on my guard.

Of course not all men are predators, but the problem we have as women is that we can never tell which one is or isn't. The guy who assaulted me on the ferry worked on the ship, he was a uniformed steward, and a courteous one at that. A very polite predator. He opened the door saying, "Come, let me help you." Those were his exact and only words. The only thing I said to him was "thank you" as I entered the bathroom. He molested me in silence. I've often wondered how many women he assaulted over the course of his career. He had the perfect MO. His victims would never be heard over the roar of the wind, and like me, would be too sick to lodge a complaint.

These were minor incidents in the scheme of things, but for me they changed everything. I realized my mother was right: the world isn't safe for girls and women. But unlike my mother I was not prepared to accept it. In fact, I was wild with indignation. Thankfully, at the same time I started to realize my own freedom to think for myself: to see through the insanity and injustice of these conditions arbitrarily imposed on females, and to take action to change them. Women's freedom was a political issue. I was 24 years old and I had woken up. I returned to Canada, finished my degree and began working in the women's shelter. My analysis continued to deepen as I was forced to reckon with the hard truth that women are neither safe in the public domain nor in the home.

I was just coming to terms with the societal scourge of intimate partner violence (and the complicity of police and courts) when I met Helen Levine, and the earth shifted again. I began to recognize the family itself as a site of injustice to women – whether there was violence or not.

The institution of motherhood – again, to be distinguished from the *experience* of motherhood – is fraught with problems, beginning with its foundational assumptions about how 'normal' women should think, feel and behave. It is presumed that motherhood comes instinctually to women; that women have an inherent desire and ability to nurture and raise children. The institution imposes an unattainable prescription for perfection on women. Selflessness is the name of the game. Mothers are not meant to have a self and are judged, and judge themselves, against standards of perfect love and endless giving. All mothers will eventually be found more or less guilty of failing their children. "It is she, finally, who is held accountable for her children's health, the clothes they wear, their behaviour at school, their intelligence and general development" (Rich 1976, p. 53). And needless to say, for their staying alive.

I had seen my own mother diminished and degraded by the institution. Left alone to clean the house and do the laundry while the family went off to their interesting lives every morning, is it any wonder she grew increasingly depressed? I cringe thinking about how I treated her at times when the beds were not made or she didn't get up to make breakfast.

Motherhood had been little explored until Adrienne Rich opened it up to intellectual scrutiny. "We know more about the air we breathe, the seas we travel, than about the nature and meaning of motherhood," she wrote (Rich 1976, p. 11). Beginning with her own experience as a young mother who yearned to write but had three sons to care for, Rich exposed the ambivalence, struggle and rage that often lies at the heart of motherhood. Her groundbreaking work allows women to make sense of confusing contradictions and resentments.

Today there are endless books, institutes, courses and discourses on motherhood and on the perils of good mother ideologies. But if research and practice is not rooted in feminist theory, that is, in women's real-life experience and its relationship to the power structure, it risks doing more harm than good. In the absence of a feminist critique, insight into the perils of the 'good mother' will inevitably lead to more woman-blaming. If she can't get over her guilt and just 'do less', 'let go', 'be less controlling', the fault will lie with her. Women who are unable to will themselves out of the institution will continue to be pathologized.

Adrienne Rich wrote *Of Woman Born* in 1976. Is her analysis outdated? Here are the words of mothers in the year 2023 responding to the question, "What does it mean to be a mother?":

- Being a mother means being completely and totally overwhelmed (in the best possible way) by love, joy, responsibility, and selflessness.
- Being a mom means sacrificing my body, my time, my finances, my sleep, and my mental health to raise my kids, knowing it will be worth it in the end because life isn't about me anymore.
- Being a mother means to demonstrate the abundance of unconditional love that has no end.
- Being a mother means it is MY responsibility to give my children the tools they need to live a happy and meaningful life.
- A mother's love is boundless, endless, seamless, selfless – unconditional.
- What it means to be a mother is to put your own problems and issues aside and guide your children through life's adventures with a happy and positive attitude.
- Motherhood is constantly feeling guilty about SOMETHING.[55]

Let me repeat, I deeply admire mothers' sense of duty and honour. We have a lot to learn from mothers, and if we had any sense they would be running the world. Unfortunately, women's ethic of care interferes with capitalism and the industrial military complex. Putting women in charge would not be good for our war economies.

---

55 '18 Moms Describe What It Means to be a Mother'. Mom's Choice Awards. <https://www.momschoiceawards.com/blog/moms-describe-what-it-means-to-be-a-mother/>. Retrieved 27 October 2024.

It is not motherhood I seek to undermine, but the conditions in which women mother. The quotes above tell us that the institution of motherhood is alive and well. Women will continue to flounder under an institution not fit for purpose. They will continue to see themselves – and be seen – as the problem, and more labels, therapy and psychopharmaceuticals will be the result. It is the structure of motherhood that needs changing, not the mothers. It is society that needs changing, not the mothers.

Women do not have children in isolation. They have children in a world growing more unfit for human habitation by the minute. They have children in the context of poverty, war, and forced migration. They have children with men who don't stick around. They have children in the context of intimate partner violence and justice systems that couldn't care less about their lives.

Women are raising kids in homes where their partners are increasingly obsessed with online porn and increasingly interested in sex dolls as 'better than the real thing'. (See Caitlin Roper's 2022 book, *Sex Dolls, Robots and Woman Hating: The Case for Resistance* for a disturbing but important read.) These trends are devastating for women and have real life consequences for them. Acting as if these shifts in society have no impact on mothers as they try to raise their kids is naive and dangerous. Women can and will break down under these conditions.

———————————

Some feminist philosophers and scholars *are* building produc-
tively on Adrienne Rich's work. For example, narratives of
women raising children born of wartime rape have opened the
door to many more complexities regarding the conditions in
which women become mothers (Takševa 2017). A woman may
be ambivalent about mothering because she also wants a career,
or to develop her talents. Or she may be ambivalent because her
child is a product of rape, or forced marriage, or child marriage,
or an abusive relationship, or community or spousal pressure.
Or she may be carrying childhood trauma. Ambivalence is a
human response to complexity, but under the dominant ideologies of motherhood women are forced to suppress complex and
conflicting emotions. The institution of motherhood gives rise to
widespread repression of the self, hindering women's capacities
and potential.

———————

And we haven't really talked about 'wifehood' – which for many
women overlaps with motherhood – and all the patriarchal
shenanigans that go on there. Marriage is another institution
fraught with problems for women, beginning with the assumption
that in the name of tradition they will yield their name to that
of their partner. It is of course a symbolic act of erasure and
ownership. Nawal el Saadawi called motherhood a prison. She
called marriage a grave.

In most households, women's time and energy are presumed
upon by men and children, as is their affinity for doing laundry

and cleaning toilets. At the same time, the domestic sphere is massively devalued and degraded, and along with it women's contributions which for the most part remain unseen and unsung. It gets very complicated. I often hear women saying, "I wouldn't mind doing it all if he appreciated it." But even all the appreciation in the world does not make an unjust situation fair, healthy or sustainable.

The Australian writer Anna Funder brings wifehood out of the closet in *Wifedom: Mrs Orwell's Invisible Life* (Funder 2023). Funder shows how George Orwell's Oxford-educated wife, Eileen O'Shaughnessy, who made significant contributions to his work, has been written out of Orwell's life by Orwell himself (she is virtually absent in his memoirs), and out of history by his male biographers. It's a devastating read that confronts ongoing fundamental problems in the structure of marriage and the traditional family. Funder refers to patriarchy as a "planetary Ponzi scheme by which the time, work and lives of women are plundered and robbed …" (Funder 2023, p. 54).

> Patriarchy, says Funder, is … a story 'so powerful that it has replaced reality with itself'. In order to maintain itself, it must play a number on women, effecting a 'vanishing trick' to efface their hurts in order for men to look innocent (Benjamin 2023).

———————————

In the course of writing this book, an Australian woman who spent 20 years incarcerated for allegedly killing her four children was pardoned and released from prison. Described as Australia's

most notorious serial killer and a monster, Kathleen Folbigg was
originally sentenced to 40 years imprisonment, reduced to 30
years on appeal. Her case caught my attention because it turned
on the issue of maternal guilt. Ms Folbigg's feelings of guilt both
as mother and as grieving mother, set down in black and white in
her private diaries, played a key role in her 2003 conviction.

The children died over a period of ten years, their ages at
death ranging from 19 days to 18 months. Folbigg always main-
tained her innocence. A 2018 enquiry into the convictions was
unsuccessful, but advances in scientific knowledge eventually
provided compelling evidence that the children died of natural
causes related to underlying genetic and medical conditions. In
2021, petitions signed by more than 150 distinguished scientists
and doctors called on the Governor of New South Wales to
pardon her. This led to a second enquiry, which recommended
her release, and on 5 June 2023 Kathleen Folbigg was released
unconditionally.[56]

The evidence against her at trial was circumstantial. There
were no signs of human intervention in any of the babies' deaths.
There was no indication the children were smothered. There
were no child welfare reports. There were no witnesses to any
criminal behaviour. There were only the diaries, discovered by her
husband in her bedside table after she left the marriage and which
he handed over to police. Diaries wherein she agonized about
herself as a mother and blamed herself for everything. Convinced

---

56 Her convictions were overturned later that year by the New South Wales Court
    of Criminal Appeal.

of his wife's guilt, Craig Folbigg helped the police build their case against her. He refused to provide the DNA sample requested by her defence and testified against her in court. Craig said that Kathleen lost her temper with the children and "struggled with motherhood."

The diaries detail Kathleen's dark moods and contain honest admissions about her struggles as a wife and mother. She was manifestly aware of her failings and felt like the worst mother on earth. She was haunted by guilt over her children's deaths. She felt responsible, confiding in her diary that she was at times short-tempered and cruel. Though never examined by psychologists or psychiatrists at trial, her writings were used to portray her as "an unstable mother, prone to rage" (Ritchie 2023). The Crown saw the diary entries in which she talked about her struggles with motherhood as admissions of guilt.

But psychological experts who gave evidence at a later inquiry viewed the diaries as a coping mechanism for a grieving mother who had complex post-traumatic stress disorder, marriage problems and little social support (Wells 2023). It must be noted that when Kathleen was just a baby herself, her father murdered her mother, stabbing her 24 times. Kathleen was placed in the care of the state at eighteen months old. Sadly, it seems the more a woman has suffered, the easier it is to pathologize her or view her with suspicion.[57]

---

57 It's the same mechanism that makes us doubt a rape victim if we know she has been raped before. A friend who followed the case told me that when she learned Kathleen's father had murdered her mother it removed all doubt about Kathleen's guilt. Her reasoning was incorrect, as it turned out.

Dr Joanna Garstang, a pediatrician and expert in sudden infant death syndrome, said that

> … the expressions of self-blame and guilt in Ms Folbigg's diary fit with those described in the literature or that I have witnessed in my clinical and research practice. I do not consider them true confessions of guilt. Ms Folbigg is blaming herself for the deaths, she may be considering that her stress caused the deaths. This is in keeping with published literature and not of concern (Whitbourn 2023).

Dr Emma Cunliffe, a professor of law at the University of British Columbia whose research interests include expert evidence and the operation of implicit bias, has written a book about the Folbigg case (Cunliffe 2011). She admits she found the diaries "distressing and difficult to interpret" when she first read them, but gradually her opinion changed:

> Kathleen Folbigg used her diaries to record her anxieties about herself and her mothering. She articulates her own sense that she carries some responsibility for her children's deaths, and when you read some of the entries that she puts, it sounds very much like she is hinting at having harmed the children. I read the diaries now as Kathleen Folbigg blaming herself for getting frustrated, for losing her temper with her children, and feeling as if, if she had only been a better mother, perhaps the children would not have died. But that's very different from admitting that she killed the children (McDermott 2019).

Professor Cunliffe says that Kathleen Folbigg's conviction relied on "casual misogyny," "discriminatory reasoning," and "thinly veiled stereotypes about women" to depict her as an unfit mother and cast her as a killer:

> They pointed to the fact that she was leaving Sarah on Saturday mornings with family members to work at a part-time job to earn more money for the household as evidence that she didn't love Sarah, didn't want to care for her, and therefore was capable of murdering Sarah. Within a criminal case when a mother is suspected of harming children, the notion of what constitutes good mothering becomes a lot narrower, so behaviours that are seen as mundane are cast as suspicious (Ritchie 2023).

Announcing Ms Folbigg's pardon, NSW Attorney General Michael Daley said the evidence suggests the journal entries were "the writings of a depressed mother, blaming herself for the death of each child, as distinct from admissions that she murdered or otherwise harmed them" (Ritchie 2023).

———————————

Perusing media accounts of the trial, I note that little is said about Craig Folbigg and any role he may have played in his wife's state of mind. Did his behaviour in the marriage have anything to do with Kathleen's anxiety and depression? Kathleen made entries in her diary about Craig's affairs and about his constant criticism of her. He told her repeatedly she needed to lose weight. He seems to have kept her off balance in the relationship, fearful of being abandoned. Why did he refuse to submit a DNA sample to help establish if there were any genetic underpinnings to the children's deaths? He was never a suspect in the deaths; why would he not want his wife cleared if she were truly innocent? But Craig Folbigg was convinced of his wife's guilt, even after her pardon. One can have full sympathy for Craig as a father who lost four children while wondering what role he may have played in his wife feeling so terrible about herself. But Kathleen's hurts in the marriage have been effaced.

———————

Dr Garstang does not consider Kathleen Folbigg's diary entries as "true" confessions of guilt. She is speaking, of course, in context of the law and serious criminal charges, and I understand and agree with her in this context. But for me, Kathleen Folbigg's diaries do contain true confessions of guilt, and though they do not indicate criminal culpability, we must not skip too quickly past them. Kathleen Folbigg has given us a window into the guilty mind of the bereaved mother. She did not cause her children's deaths, but she suffers as if she did, accepts responsibility as if she did. Her words of self-reproach and self-loathing are identical to the words uttered by mothers of kids who have died by suicide.

I will give the last, heartbreaking word to Kathleen, who I think speaks for all mothers:

> You've got to understand that those diaries are written from the point of me always blaming myself. I blamed myself for everything. It's just I took so much of the responsibility, because that's, as mothers, what you do (Dalton 2023).

Chapter 5

The Power of Women Talking

But I was a good mother

> We are wasting time … by passing this burden, this sack of stones, from one to the next, by pushing our pain away. We mustn't do this. We mustn't play Hot Potato with our pain. Let's absorb it ourselves, each of us … Let's inhale it, let's digest it, let's process it into fuel.
>
> —Miriam Toews

> Lock up your libraries if you like; but there is no gate, no lock, no bolt that you can set upon the freedom of my mind.
>
> —Virginia Woolf

How is the freedom of the mind relevant to the heartbroken mother of the suicided child? How, in a book about a subject so tender, so devastating, so emotionally charged, can I justify exhorting women to think? If I were a mother who had lost a child to suicide, I might be inclined to use some very strong language in response to this suggestion. That's how I felt about the Lucy Stone poster.

From where I sit, it is a matter of going where the argument leads. In this book, I have tried to be true to what I have seen and heard in my life and work. For nearly four decades I have been listening to and learning from women. I've witnessed enough gratuitous suffering to sicken me to eternity. I have seen the futility of trying to assist women without considering the power structures bearing down upon our lives. I stopped working that way a long time ago.

To be sure, thinking is not the only matter that needs addressing. There are other things that must be said, and as I hold the pen, I plan to say them. There are things we can do to support women so catastrophically bereaved. There is also a scathing indictment to be made of society itself for its cataclysmic failure to mothers.

But if all I can do in this book is to offer one opinion it would be this: women need to seriously engage with the power of our own minds. We need to start thinking about our own situation, which is indeed dire. Our own clear thinking is the axis upon which this whole story will turn.

A mother whose child dies by suicide may eventually stop feeling guilty 'on her own', as it were, without an analytical (feminist) framework to guide her. But she will relinquish her guilt not as a matter of principle, but because she is tired; because she has grown weary of it; because she has come to terms with its futility. She may feel better to be rid of it, but she will not likely be stronger. Strength comes from a clear-eyed recognition of the subordinate status imposed on all women. Strength comes from a principled refusal of the guilt fostered in females from cradle to grave.

"I'm done with the guilt," a mother says to me, nearly two decades after her daughter's suicide. Then in the next breath: "I have no self-esteem left." Her low self-esteem is an indication that she is not on solid ground despite hospitalization and years of therapy and prescription drugs.

I want mothers on solid ground. I want them to feel okay about themselves even as they struggle with catastrophic loss. Suffering and self-esteem are not mutually exclusive, in fact a strong sense of self is an asset when pain and loss are everywhere. The work of grief demands confidence that one's own life and suffering are of value. It demands being able to ask for what we need, confident that we will not be abandoned in the process. It demands clarity of thought, and a voice. Women are poorly positioned for this work. Getting ourselves in position is the subject of this chapter. When we make connections with other women, we begin to find our bearings.

In *Women Talking,* eight women climb into a hayloft to discuss some very serious matters. Though they are in distress they do not go to the psychiatrist's office. They go to the hayloft because they recognize their problem is not personal but political.[58] They go to the hayloft, a private space where they can talk without fear of being ridiculed, pathologized or silenced. They go the hayloft

---

58 'The personal is political' expresses the feminist concept that women's personal experiences are rooted in larger social and political structures and gender inequality.

where they can think for themselves, about themselves. No one can or should do this thinking for them.

The women engage in a feminist process, placing their own pain and fear into the centre of the room. They put words on the unsayable, facing up to disturbing truths about their lives. The way they have been brutalized. The way they have been duped, maligned, spun as crazy. The way they have been complicit. How much they have given yet how little they have received. How little they have asked for. How little they have mattered. Everything is on the table: faith, tradition, justice, forgiveness, their own rage; their desire to be good people. Hope. A vision of a different world.

It's not an easy conversation. They're not all on the same page. Some are fighters. Some are dreamers. Some are more pragmatic. Tempers flare. There is eye rolling and the occasional 'fuck you'. But they stay in the conversation and they hash it out, supportively, with humour, never backing away from the complexities. The dialogue continues over two days. They are at a crossroads and must decide whether they continue to accept the conditions imposed on them, or take a different path. The stakes couldn't be higher.

I think mothers are at a similar crossroads. As are all women. We all live in a patriarchy, we're all in trouble, and we all need to get to the hayloft, and fast, for some serious conversations.

———————

As I was writing this book I was often asked, "But what about the fathers?" Of course I recognize that the fathers are suffering too. The struggle to come to terms with unbearable pain and unalterable circumstances is not essentially 'gendered'. The father of the suicided child also has a profound struggle on his hands, and my heart goes out to him. But *the struggle itself,* the existential crisis is not my primary concern. There are plenty of books on the struggle itself.[59]

My concern is with what we might call 'the politics of women's grief': the place where a mother's human suffering intersects with her condition under the system of patriarchy. Living in a male-defined and dominated world undermines women's strength, confidence and capacities. In a world where men are the meaning-makers, women are deprived of language itself, the primary tool to grasp our own experience. We lack words and concepts to understand our own reality.

I know it's hard for a mother to think about her own life when her child has died by suicide. Her own life is the last thing on her mind, indeed, she may not even want to live, nor feel entitled to live. I recognize I'm treading on sacred ground here and I want to stress before venturing further that I take the depth of a mother's despair and self-condemnation very seriously. I know she will

---

59 Among my favourites is *Man's Search for Meaning,* the pioneering work of psychiatrist and Holocaust survivor Viktor Frankl who teaches us that meaning can be found in even the most desolate of locations. "Everything can be taken from a man [sic] but one thing: the last of human freedoms – to choose one's attitude in any given set of circumstances, to choose one's own way" (Frankl 1985).

have to go at her own pace. But I want to push the envelope by suggesting that a mother is entitled to survive the suicide of her child and to thrive as a human being, albeit a very changed one. She is entitled to pick up her life; to feel okay about getting on with building, or rebuilding, a meaningful life.

I can tell you from working in a trauma unit, not all our kids are going to make it. A mother must not spend the rest of her life in a state of atonement for a crime she did not commit. I want her to have the dignity of a struggle that is not undermined by spurious charges of inadequate mothering. She needs all her resources to cope with her loss. But patriarchy and its capricious cruelties are not going away anytime soon, so I am afraid she will have to get herself to the hayloft and struggle alongside other mothers who have lost a child to suicide. They will all have similar anxieties and questions.

———————————

For me, the hayloft has become a metaphor for a place where women can speak truthfully about our own lives without fear of retribution. Suppression, censorship and pretending are survival skills mastered by the world's women. We censor ourselves to keep the peace; to keep our own pain at bay; because nobody much cares what we think anyway; and because saying what we think can be very dangerous. The hayloft is a place where women can cease pretending. It is a dynamic, relational space, full of movement and potential. It is a place of care, compassion, humour and healing. It is a place to think and speak, listen and be heard; to face up to the world as it is and to envision a different world. It's a place for dreamers and realists alike. It is my favourite place on earth.

———————

It so happens that I found myself in a hayloft this week, in the kitchen of an acquaintance whom I will call Ruth. Ruth's friend was also present; I will call her Anne. Ruth had contacted me asking for advice for Anne, whose daughter is not doing well. Also in the house was Ruth's husband, whom she quickly dispatched, closing the kitchen door behind him. He retreated to his second-floor study, quite cheerfully it seemed. Men aren't really interested in women's conversations anyway. Still, we can't talk openly when they are around.

As Ruth poured coffee Anne described her daughter's situation, one I have heard so often I could write the script. It's the classic nightmare of a mother trying to protect herself and her children after leaving an abusive marriage. There is ongoing stalking and intimidation. The kids are fearful of their father and don't want to see him. The father has been successful at spinning his children's antipathy towards him as 'parental alienation' by their mother. Revictimized by the courts, in debt to lawyers, dealing with angry kids, fearful of her ex, Anne's daughter is on the verge of collapse.[60]

---

60   It is typical in these situations that the kids take out their anger and disappointment on their mother. The mother not only absorbs her children's distress but is forced to work even harder to make up for the father's destructive behaviour.

What do I have to offer these women? There is nothing I can do to change what's happening. By the time such mothers get to me they have exhausted all avenues of recourse: switching lawyers (thinking that's the problem); requesting a more experienced child protection worker (thinking that's the problem); maneuvering to a more experienced judge (thinking that's the problem.) What I *can* do is open up the space so that the women can see what's happening to Anne's daughter in context. So that the patterned and deliberate nature of the injustice to women becomes visible. And that is what I did, using some tough examples from my work. The women in the kitchen – their hayloft – were astonished to realize that this can really be happening in Canada in the 2020s; that mothers trying to protect their children are routinely forsaken by our courts.

We sat in silence. Ruth poured another round of coffee. Suddenly I felt very self-conscious, thinking maybe I'd gone too far. I should speak less, listen more; not tell the worst stories. Why do I have to tell the worst stories? I should leave out the murders …

"I'm sorry," I said. "I hope I haven't depressed you too much." Ruth smiled:

It's been a difficult conversation, but I'm feeling really good! Really energized! It's relieving to hear the truth spoken! To have words put on experiences that we spend so much time pushing away, trying to deny. Can we do this again?!

Ruth went on to disclose some things that had surfaced for her during our conversation. Things long buried about her own struggles as a mother.

A few days later I received an email from Anne:

> Your visit awakened me to the dysfunction of the court system, that my daughter's situation is not unusual. My daughter hasn't done anything wrong, in fact, quite the contrary. So many women are unjustly treated by the patriarchal legal and police systems. So many children are in the same position as my grandsons. What are these boys learning about women, seeing their mothers being pushed around, lied to, their needs ignored, their motherly instincts ignored? I encourage you to get the truth out there. Women need what you write to be heard and read. It is valuable beyond words.

The hayloft had worked its magic. But it wasn't just Anne and Ruth who were energized. I was as well. Not a big surprise. I've been meeting women in small groups for decades and typically come away feeling great. People often ask me how I can do this work. "It's so depressing," they say. I've never found it that way. Not from day one. Where truth is spoken there is energy and light, and creativity. At least you have a fighting chance. But I noted that I was even more energized than usual. Since seeing *Women Talking* at the cinema and reading the book, there has been a dramatic opening in my own imagination.

I've always called what I do 'group work'. I've never, ever called it 'therapy', because the word connotes pathology and illness, implying that there is something fundamentally wrong that needs fixing. I have always seen my work as more political than psychological. It's society that is fundamentally broken, not women. But *Women Talking* takes group work to another level. Something radical happens in that hayloft. The women think. They plan. Then they act. With conviction. They are scared to death but confident at the same time, guided by their own knowing. Enough is enough, they're moving on. Moving to a new world where they and their daughters will no longer be policed, devalued, victimized, shamed, silenced. They know the world they want and they are moving towards it.

But how do they know another world is possible? They know it from inside their own lives. They know because they have lived it in the hayloft; in the company of other women. It occurs to me that every time we are in the hayloft we are not just imagining a different world, we are *in* that world. We have built it and we are in it. Maybe the hayloft *is* the world that women imagine and long for. The women's 'up and leaving' symbolizes women moving on from patriarchal thought, with all its prescriptions, proscriptions and violence. It's an extraordinary act of liberation.

It all begins with knowing.[61] Knowing something is very wrong. Knowing something else is possible. For many years I thought the knowing experienced by mothers who have lost a child to suicide was connected to their grief. I still think this is largely true. Only another mother can understand the life-threatening dimensions of this grief. But I'm beginning to suspect that the women's knowing is also tied to their shared suffering

---

61   Definitions of knowing point to a state of being aware, or even keenly, shrewdly, astutely aware; of being informed; of possessing exclusive or 'insider' knowledge.

under patriarchy and the institution of motherhood. They may not have words for it, but I hazard a guess that all mothers know at some level that the conditions in which they bear and raise children are not woman-centred, have not been created in their interest, and are often unjust. I suspect that at some level all mothers know that they are unjustly blamed.

An outstanding example of women's knowing can be found in the short story *A Jury of Her Peers* (1927) by Susan Glaspell, a classic tale of a woman's experience before the law. The setting is an isolated farmhouse in rural USA. A woman named Minnie Wright has been arrested on suspicion of murdering her husband and is being held in the county jail. The sheriff, the district attorney and a neighbour attend the farmhouse to investigate the murder, accompanied by two of the men's wives who are tasked with collecting Mrs Wright's personal effects. The women remain in the kitchen while the men go about the work of gathering evidence to support a murder charge. Intent on finding some sort of recognizable inducement for violence, the men come up empty-handed. It is the women who solve the murder by piecing together the clues in the kitchen; clues which point to loneliness and neglect and a woman silenced throughout her marriage. The women read depression in the state of the kitchen, and interpret a piece of sewing where neat stitching suddenly turns erratic as a sign that Minnie Wright had suffered a mental shock. They are also able to perceive the signs of a husband's rage: a broken bird cage, the door twisted off its hinges; a strangled bird carefully wrapped in satin and hidden in a sewing basket. The women recognize Minnie Wright as an abused woman pushed to the breaking point. They know she does not stand a chance of a fair trial, and in a wordless act of female solidarity, they hide the evidence that would convict her: the bird with a broken neck.

How do they know Minnie Wright is a woman deserving of compassion, not punishment, even in the face of such a terrible deed? They know it from inside their own lives:

> I might 'a' known she needed help! I tell you, it's queer, Mrs Peters. We live close together, and we live far apart. We all go through the same things – it's all just a different kind of the same thing! If it weren't – why do you and I understand? Why do we know – what we know this minute? (Glaspell 1927, p.10)

———————

On the other hand, what is it that the men – the sheriff, the district attorney and the neighbour – don't know; cannot know; cannot discern? Why are they unable to look with open hearts and minds into the life of a woman? They are not bad men, but they are men all the same, and – as it stands – they have a very different way of seeing. They occupy a different world, and unfortunately have come to believe in the superiority of that world and their own importance in it. Contemptuous of the kitchen as the domain of women – and therefore of trifling thought and activity – the men miss the central clues to the murder.

But even had they seen the clues they could not have interpreted them, for their sense of their own importance has led to moral blindness. They know the world only from their own perspective. It wouldn't be such a problem if they didn't confuse their point of view with truth itself. Simone de Beauvoir (1949) writes: "Representation of the world, like the world itself, is the work of men; they describe it from their own point of view, which they confuse with the absolute truth."

It wouldn't be such a problem if they did not stand as judge and jury over women's lives.

Unfortunately, women too often confuse men's representations for truth itself, overriding our own instincts; deferring to the male prerogative to name and proclaim. Women live in a world that for all intents and purposes does not include or represent us, yet defines our experiences as if it did. Those meanings are rarely accurate, yet we proceed in life, law and love as if they were. Is it any wonder that disappointment is the lot of women? How can life but fail to disappoint under these conditions?

———————

I turn on CBC radio this morning to get the weather.[62] I haven't even had coffee and they're talking about the normalization of choking in teen sexual activity. Eighty per cent of students surveyed at an American university report having experienced 'rough sex'. Females are overwhelmingly on the receiving end of

---

62   The Canadian Broadcasting Corporation (CBC) is Canada's national public broadcaster.

the violence. Fully two-thirds of female respondents reported being choked during sex.[63]

The researcher describes sexual choking as a form of strangulation, cutting off air and/or blood flow to the brain by applying pressure to the neck. Hands, forearm, belt or ligature may be used. She attributes the normalization of sexual choking to ubiquitous internet memes and online porn.

What's driving the trend? *A reaction to the advancements of women's rights*, she opines.

A second researcher reports that in a focus group of girls aged fourteen to seventeen, participants identified that they lacked the capacity to say 'no' to the pressure to engage in rough sex. The girls also reported feeling constrained in basic social situations such as choosing a movie, unable to express their own wishes and preferences. The girls are afraid to use their own voice, fearful of the consequences should they come across as prudish, needy, difficult or 'high maintenance'. So they learn to fake agreement and consent.

Of all the horrors talked about in this 25-minute segment, including the serious adverse effects and long-term consequences of sexual strangulation (brain injury, stroke, cardiac arrest and even death), what jumps out at me is that teenage girls are fearful of using their own voice. They are just kids and already silencing themselves, their personal power draining away with every act of

---

63   'Why your teen might think rough sex is the norm', *CBC Radio*, 9 May 2024. <https://www.cbc.ca/listen/live-radio/1-63-the-current/clip/16064829-why-teen-might-think-rough-sex-norm>.

self-abnegation. How is this going to play out when they enter the complicated lands of wifedom and motherhood? How will not having a voice play out when the going gets tough?

Like the protagonists in *Women Talking* they will keep trucking along, avoiding painful truths, oblivious to the power structure, accepting the conditions assigned to them – until something happens to ignite their rage.

Who exactly are we as women? We are the ones who just get on with it, adapting, accommodating, acquiescing, trying to please, grateful for any bones thrown our way. Keeping our expectations low so we won't be disappointed. Smiling and saying 'thank you' after we have been hurt. Until something happens to ignite the smouldering fire. Until something happens that is so enormous and so extreme it cannot be managed using the usual methods.

This 'igniting' *could* be a moment of reckoning with all that has been buried, lost, seized, plundered, surrendered, denied, forfeited. It could be a moment for drawing a line in the sand. Alas, in the absence of a feminist framework, women turn the energy inward, and tear ourselves to shreds.

I suspect that for a mother, her child's death by suicide ignites a certain terror deep inside her.[64] Something beyond the loss itself.

---

64   It must not be lost on us that a synonym for terror is monster.

It has to do with a lifetime of not having a voice. It has to do with the institution of motherhood, that has set her up for failure. It has to do with the gap between all she has given and how little her contributions have been valued.

It has to do with loneliness and not being seen. It has to do with all those nights when the kids were sick and she was by herself and scared. It has to do with all the slights and injustices swallowed along the way.

It has to do with the circumstances in which she became a mother. The fact that she never wanted kids, or had to fight like hell to have them, or wanted more, or is an adoptive mother.

It has to do with other children lost. A pregnancy terminated through necessity or force. A baby miscarried. A stillbirth. Losses not sufficiently mourned because there wasn't time, or it wasn't safe, or because such losses aren't considered that significant. Or simply because there can never be adequate mourning for a child.

It has to do with trauma carried from her own childhood.

It has to do with how deeply she loved her child, and how very hard she tried.

It has to do with the Trojan Horse that arrived the moment she learned of her child's suicide, penetrating her defences; its corrupting messages of blame spilling into her life with cunning and power.

We know that depression is often anger turned inward. I suspect that women's debilitating guilt is our own powerlessness turned inward.

Changing the unjust conditions of women's lives is a long-term project. We need to be on solid ground for the fight. First and foremost we need our sanity. Seeing clearly, naming things accurately, restores sanity and self-worth, putting us on firm footing. We need to take control of our own lives and the narrative of our lives. We will do this by coming together in small groups to name and resist the unjust conditions imposed upon us, beginning with patriarchy's false naming:

> Women have been driven mad, 'gaslighted', for centuries by the refutation of our experience and our instincts in a culture which validates only male experience. … Women have often felt insane when cleaving to the truth of our experience. Our future depends on the sanity of each of us, and we have a profound stake, beyond the personal, in the project of describing our reality as candidly and fully as we can to each other (Rich 1979, p. 190).

It's to the hayloft for all of us. We will need haylofts everywhere, in every community, for every subject and every problem. Wherever there are women we will need haylofts so we can compare notes and develop clarity of thought and plans for action. In every situation there are real choices to be made, and real power to be had.

———————————

Can a woman reclaim her shattered motherhood on her own? Maybe some can. But if you're asking my opinion, this is not a journey for a woman to make alone. It's just too hard.

"Mothers need other mothers," as Kate said. Women need other women. For real and lasting change to occur, the work of our own liberation must be done in concert with other women.

The mother who has lost a child to suicide will be joined in the hayloft by other mothers in the same situation. She may have to be helped up the ladder because she lacks the energy to climb it herself. A hand from above, a leg up from below. Once there, she will find the kettle on. They will make her a cup of tea, place a box of tissues beside her, and she will relax into their knowing. The mothers will hold her and say, "We know. We know."

After a while they will show her photographs of their kids and tell her what happened, and she will hang on to their every word. And then she will take out a picture of her child and tell them what happened, and they will hang on to her every word. And as they compare notes she will begin to recognize how much these women loved their kids, how much they gave, how hard they tried; how difficult the circumstances were.

In their love and devotion to their children who didn't make it, she will begin to remember her love for and devotion to her own child: how much she gave, how hard she tried, how difficult the circumstances were. And when she notices them slipping into self-laceration she will not let them go under, because she knows – from the inside of her own life – the unreasonableness and injustice of their guilt. She will extend to them the compassion she is unable to extend to herself. She will not allow the other mothers to drown in the same dark waters that are overwhelming her, and in saving them, she will save herself.

Gradually, in the company of other women, she will begin to have compassion for herself. In the faces of the other women, in their stories, in their love and in the pain they carry, the true story of motherhood, and her motherhood, is reflected back to her. Bit by bit she will reclaim the goodness and integrity of her relationship with her deceased child. Bit by bit she will take back her shattered motherhood. She is on solid footing now, because *this* is reality. The mirror that patriarchy held up to her is a distortion, a fiction. The truth is, she was a good enough mother.

Chapter 6

Lessons from a Police Crisis Unit

Never separate a mother from her child

In my work with the police I accompanied many mothers who lost a child in traumatic circumstances. These were searing moments of grief and despair, at times explosive and frightening, at times quiet and tender; always sacred. What is this force that seems to pull to the heart of life itself? What is this bond between mother and child that, when severed, threatens the mother's own life?

On one level, it's obvious. "She's the mother," people will say, "of course she's going to have her heart ripped out when she loses a child." But there are contradictions. If we recognize the significance of the mother-child bond, why do we as a society not do more to nurture and sustain it? Why are our mothers under-resourced and under-valued? Why do we entrap mothers with abusive men? Why do our family courts separate children from their mothers as if it's of little consequence? Why are mothers who are forced to flee across international borders to protect their children viewed as kidnappers under the Hague Convention?[65]

---

65   "Under The Hague Convention on the Civil Aspects of International Child Abduction 1980, a child is considered abducted if they are taken across international borders by one parent without the other parent's consent. The motive

Given all that mothers give, sacrifice and suffer in their maternal role, why aren't we taking better care of them?

I ask Kate if she thinks we, as a society, honour mothers. "There's a recognition, but it doesn't go deep," she says. "I've never read anything specifically about mothers losing a child to suicide. There's a reason for that. We don't honour mothers. We don't think about them."

———

For a mother, the death of a child under any circumstances is unbearable. When the child is severed from the mother's life by his or her own hand, the cleaving is particularly brutal. It is a bereavement with no equivalence in human experience. The psychological sequelae are deep, complex and long lasting.

---

for taking the child is not relevant. Over 100 countries have signed the treaty. The Convention, originally aimed at abducting fathers, was designed to ensure the quick and safe return of the child. In that regard, the treaty is highly effective. Now, however, around 75% of the parents who are brought before the courts are mothers. And many of them are fleeing domestic violence, trying to get to safety in their home country with their child. The cases are brought by the perpetrators of that violence with support from the state. In a majority of cases, even when there is clear evidence of violence or criminality by the father, the Convention insists that the child must be returned. As the child's primary carer, most mothers return too – in spite of the very real risks to their safety. Their situation is now precarious in the extreme. They face an escalation of violence and abuse from the child's father, and economic hardship and potential homelessness if they try to leave the relationship. Labelled by the courts as a child abductor and kidnapper, mothers are branded a risk to their own children. Should there subsequently be a custody battle, as there often is, this puts them at a serious disadvantage in the custody case they will then have to fight in a foreign court." <https://www.hague-mothers.org.uk/about/>. Retrieved 14 September 2024.

The mother who has worked so hard to preserve the life of her child is now abandoned by that child. The child, in rejecting their own life, rejects the mother. The sense of having failed and being responsible is off the charts. The mother's location in society makes everything so much harder. Lack of a strong psychological infrastructure, lack of agency, lack of voice and language contribute to her invisibility and isolation.

To be seen in our pain is a deeply human need. When we are suffering we need to be seen by others, and, to be seen, we need a voice; we have to be able to tell our own story. Language is the vehicle by which we give and receive compassion. We have to be able to tell our own story, and we need thoughtful, caring people to receive it. This is where an informed community can help. There are things we can do to ease a mother's pain.

In this chapter I lay out some lessons learned in my time working with the police service. They are insights gained from crisis intervention and at first glance may seem most relevant for first responders or those present in the immediate suicide crisis. But if we comprehend all that a mother must navigate in the initial phase of the trauma, we will have insight into what she needs for the long haul.

And if the lessons are truly understood they can be game changers, for embedded in them are the fundamental conditions of women's lives. They highlight the barriers all women face in trying to be seen and heard. If we understand all that a mother must navigate to cope with her child's suicide, we will by extension understand what all women living under patriarchy are up against.

———————

1. Never separate a grieving mother from her child

The mother will probably want and need to be with her child's body. I have seen distraught mothers become calm when allowed contact with their son or daughter. I say 'allowed' because sudden deaths are frequently accompanied by a police investigation which may be compromised by contact with the deceased. Police and coroner may be reluctant to allow anyone to touch the body. Advocate for the mother. This moment cannot be taken back. Even if a mother can hold her child's hand it can soothe her. Even being in the room with her child can help. If the child's body is in a bad condition the mother must be cautioned and carefully prepared. Steps can be taken to cover visible injuries. But whether she sees the child must be her decision.

2. Help her figure out what she needs and give it to her

Do not presume that a mother in these circumstances will be able to know or articulate her needs. She may never before have been asked to say what she wants. Her honest feelings may be behind multiple barriers and not within reach. Give her time to figure it out. If she says she doesn't need anything, give her more time. Keep opening up the space so she can access her own voice.

3. Slow things down

This moment cannot be revisited. Mistakes or omissions cannot be undone. In this initial stage of cleaving, a mother may experience herself as split wide open, or having a limb severed, or alternatively not being in her body at all. Where there is a police investigation, things can move very quickly in the direction of the law and legal processes and human needs can get short shrift. Slow things down. Give the mother time to absorb the first terrible wave. Give her as much time with her child as she wants. Ask her if she wants to be alone with her child.

4. Centre the mother in your interventions

Put the mother at the centre of events. This is not to say that fathers should not receive full care and support. It is simply to honour the mother's distinct relationship with her child. She is experiencing her child's death and her own death at the same time. Remember that when the child dies, the mother dies too.

5. Do not pathologize her reactions

Do not rush to medicate or subdue her. Just be with her. Quietly. A hand on her back to ground her. Follow her cues. Help her with her breathing. The first waves of emotion will be torrential but need to be expressed. It is critical that we depathologize women's legitimate responses to extreme pain and trauma.

6. Do not patronize her

If a mother wants to go to the site where her child died, or to the place where her child's body has been taken, be it a hospital or morgue, she needs to be taken there. Even if it 'doesn't make sense'. Even if it 'might upset her'. There is a tendency to be paternalistic with women ("You don't want to see that") or protective ("You don't want to remember her this way") or practical ("You won't be able to see him, anyway"). Again, never separate a grieving mother from her child.

7. Be alert to power dynamics that may silence or exclude her

I'm thinking of situations where a husband will speak on behalf of himself and his wife, for example, "No, we don't want to see our daughter's body." Or it could be religious or cultural norms or practices that prevent a mother from being with her child. Take her aside if necessary. Being given due respect as the mother, honouring her role and her agency will be a gift to her. She may decide that she doesn't want to see her child but it will be *her* decision. Not having to push against a controlling partner or oppressive cultural norms will preserve precious energy. Conversely, being disregarded may cause serious emotional harm. I have seen mothers carry scars long into the future from being sidelined at this time.

8. Make sure the mother is notified, and as soon as possible

I have seen situations where no one has thought to include the mother, or where a decision has been made to exclude her. For a mother to be shut out of her child's suicide is a non-starter. She must be given the opportunity to come to the site if logistically possible. She must know what is happening as it is happening and be given the opportunity to participate in whatever way she can in her child's last moments.

9. The mother's pain will be intense. Accompany her

The pain will visit her in waves over the coming days, weeks, months, years. We need to make space for it. It can be scary to witness. She herself may not be sure she will survive it. But the agony needs to be released, and accompanying the mother in her anguish is what she needs from us. Remember that guilt exacerbates the pain and needs to be expressed and explored. We need to make space for her anger too, an emotion not readily tolerated in women.

10. If there are siblings present, reassure them

We tend to want mothers to pull it together so as not to upset the other kids. Instead we need to explain to the children what is happening to their mother, reassuring them that she is going to be okay, she is just in a lot of pain right now. Then take them to another room or a place nearby with a caring adult to tend to them. They are massively upset too, and seeing their mother off the rails is frightening and may trigger feelings of insecurity or anger. Others must step in to look after the children, freeing the mother to focus single-mindedly – and without guilt – on her deceased child. Support for the siblings following a suicide is a topic unto itself, but I touch on it here as part of looking at what mothers need.

11. Give her time off to grieve and shower her with support

There are no benefits for mothers: no medical leave, no bereavement leave, no time off at all. A mother injured in the line of duty is expected to just keep going, still expected to function as primary caretaker in the family. What she really needs is to be relieved of her duties and to be on the receiving end of care without having to worry that she will be abandoned or made to pay a price for looking after herself. It is important to understand that her sense of motherhood has been shattered by her child's suicide and she may feel even more pressure to step up to the plate as mother to her other children. Her fear of rejection will likely be very high right now and she may feel the need to prove herself worthy. This is where an informed, supportive partner and community can make all the difference. The father is grieving too of course, but special consideration for the mother is essential.

12. Continue to keep the mother at the centre of care and concern

This is advice for the long haul. Keep opening up the space so the mother can find her own words to name and explore her suffering and ask for what she needs. Listen and receive without judgement whatever she has to say. All control has been taken away from her. Pain and self-recrimination may continue unabated for years. A mother carries her own sorrow and guilt, the judgement of the community, the suffering of her deceased child, and the fallout from the suicide among her surviving children. She has a lot on her plate. She needs her family and friends to understand and stay close.

———————————

A 62-year-old UK woman named Pat whose son died in a motorcycle accident poignantly expresses the distinct needs of the bereaved mother. Pat participated in a study at Oxford University that examined the value of viewing the body of a loved one after a traumatic death. Her struggle to express her own needs, and the undermining by her ex-husband, are textbook:

> I couldn't have borne not to have seen him … We needed to see him … And then I asked if I could go back in to see my son on my own. Because I knew then I wanted to touch him. … And my ex-husband frowned at me and obviously didn't want me to … He looked at me as he might a child saying, 'Are you going to behave yourself?' And I said, 'Look, I'm not going to do anything silly, I just want to be with him again'. And so I went back in. But of course the coroner's officer, and I guess it's … a rule of some sort, but she came in to the place with me and was standing on the other side of a glass … where she could see me the whole time. So I wasn't allowed to be with Matthew, with my son on my own. I wasn't allowed to be. And I am sorry about that and I don't understand why it is that a mother cannot be with her child on her own if that's what she wishes. I don't understand why I could not have, I could not have washed him, I could not have dressed him, I could not have looked after him and done that for him … looked after him in that way as I did when he came into the world, and when he was helpless. And I, I would have wanted to do that. And I understand that many people wouldn't and couldn't but I would have wanted to do that …

Interviewer: "Did you ask to be left alone?"
Pat:

> I didn't, I didn't. I couldn't find my voice. At all. I couldn't, I couldn't,
> I couldn't find my voice. … I really would ask for more under-
> standing, particularly for mothers who have carried their children
> inside themselves and have given birth to them and have loved them
> and cared for them through their lives. And no matter how much of
> an adult their children are when they die, mothers particularly still
> want and need to care for their children.[66]

———————

I write to Kate asking for more words. How can we better support
a mother following her child's suicide? Here is her response:

> Be present for me, don't disappear altogether, keep showing up. Have
> no/low expectations. I'm not able to plan ahead or deal with too
> many strangers or crowds. Cover for me as needed, if, say, a sunny
> stranger wants to engage and I'm simply unable to respond in kind.
> Whatever you do, do not say, "Let me know if there's anything I can
> do." That puts the burden on me to reach out and be vulnerable.
> Instead, call me up and say, "I'm going for a walk in an hour, would
> you like to come?" Or suggest a chat over coffee. Share a good book
> idea, or even just send a text that tells me you're thinking of me.

---

66 'Bereavement due to traumatic death'. <https://healthtalk.org/bereavement-
due-traumatic-death/>. Database of Individual Patient Experiences or DIPEx.
Website is <health.org>. It's a project run by Dipex Charity (Direct Patient
Experience) in partnership with the Health Experiences Research Group
at Oxford University. Pat's interview is found at <https://healthtalk.org/
interviewees/pat-interview-05/>.

Simple things that don't require much of me but mean so much and help me get through the days. Some days these gestures literally got me out of bed.

Support mothers. Ask them what they need. Give them whatever they need during difficult and traumatic times. Provide them with liberal time off.

Any escape to a soothing respite would help. A place where one would be treated gently, taken care of, removed from the harsh realities of life to come together and be cocooned, supported, given time to start to heal.

Keep saying Theo's name. Tell me your memories of him. Remind me that he mattered and was loved. Whenever anyone speaks about Theo in any form, to reminisce, to recall a funny anecdote or just to reiterate how sad they are and how much they miss him too, it makes me feel less crazy and alone. Don't be afraid to talk about him or how he died. I am already thinking of him 24/7 so it's not as if you are going to raise difficult feelings. They are already there, you're just making it safe for me to talk them through when you bring up his name.

Stop blaming and stigmatizing mothers for their children's suicides.

Chapter 7

Atonement: A Feminist Reversal

I began to think about atonement following an encounter with a woman whose son had taken his own life many years before. She is a grandmother now, pushing a couple of kids in a stroller and holding another by the hand. She didn't look great, I thought, and seemed weary, heavy of heart. At the time of her child's suicide she had been a successful professional with a full, dynamic life. These days she devotes herself to helping her remaining child by looking after her grandkids.

I came away from that meeting troubled. What was it? I couldn't put my finger on it. Plenty of women look after their grandchildren, and it can be a great source of fulfillment. It's certainly no secret that it can be exhausting. It can also be complicated, another institution laden with presumptions and assumptions about what women should do and give. Maybe I'd just caught her on a bad day.

But there was something else. It finally occurs to me. *Atonement.* What I was seeing was atonement. Twenty years later this mother is still doing penance for having failed as a mother. I feel all the old protective feelings for mothers surfacing in me, going off like a fire alarm at the first hint of smoke. Atonement is an offshoot, or derivative of guilt. If the guilt's not right for the mother of the suicided child, then neither is the atonement.

Atonement is a strong word. Definitions centre around reparation for a sin, injury, crime or wrongdoing committed. Inherent in the concept is the idea that the wrongdoer is very bad, unclean, defiled. A sinner. A felon.

Once again, the picture is complicated, because at first glance atonement seems like a good thing. How can you go wrong with an emotion that seeks to put things right? All humans make mistakes; isn't it healthy to want to make reparation? The desire to atone can guide us toward more ethical behaviour, motivating us to repair relationships with each other and with the community. I suspect this mother's desire to atone for her child's suicide comes from a very noble place within her: from love, and humility, and the high standard she has set for herself in her maternal role. We would have a much better world if more people felt this level of responsibility towards those entrusted to their care.

But is it healthy to atone where one is not blameworthy? As always, I proceed cautiously in my thinking, conscious I am still on sacred ground. Who am I to mess with a mother's grief, to interrogate her way of handling her own suffering? But I have to ask, is it healthy, that is, conducive to promoting well-being, to atone when one is not culpable? Could atonement be a form of self-punishment or self-abasement? Is atonement like guilt in that it can lead to problems if unfounded or out of proportion?

Is atonement, like guilt, sometimes political? It seems to me that if one group of people is unreasonably or disproportionately atoning, disproportionately stepping up to heal the shattered bonds of family and community, there's a problem. It seems to me that if the subordinated group is doing all the atoning, there is a problem.

I need to speak with Mary.

Mary was in the original group. She is a deep thinker who enjoys wrestling with philosophical questions. She knows I'm working on this book and has offered to help in any way she can. It has been 18 years since her daughter took her own life at the age of 18. I know that Mary carried massive guilt following Siobhan's death. I write asking if she relates to the concept of atonement. Is *she* still trying to make amends for her child's suicide? Here is her reply:

> The idea of atonement rings true for me – totally. And I feel the need to atone, quite consciously, almost all of the time. It's related to Siobhan's death for sure, but more so now to how I feel about my surviving children and needing to atone for whatever impact my failures as a mother have had on them. This has two parts – one, related to just how they are day-to-day, and two, how their sister's death has affected them (her death being caused by me). I'm using hyperbole to make a point, but that is the truth. No amount of discussion or therapy will ever relieve me of that and I'm not expecting it to because I know I failed as a mother. As a matter of fact, I truly feel almost insulted if people tell me I did all that I could. I feel that they are trying to get me to ignore the facts. When I do think of atonement directly, I have reached the point of knowing

that I can't change what's done – I'm not sure I totally accepted that for years, reliving the situation with all the 'what ifs' etc. But I do say to myself now that I can 'do good for the world' for whatever time I have left.

I find Mary's words heartbreaking. My sadness is swiftly followed by anger. Anger at a world that fosters so much suffering in women. It isn't fair, and it isn't right.

I think atonement is another trap for women. Another of patriarchy's tricks and schemes designed to keep mothers, in particular, off balance, feeling bad, focused on everything they've done wrong. Another avoidance mechanism for dealing with so much real harm done to women. Another patriarchal reversal. It is clear to me from everything I have seen that women's inordinate guilt and need to atone are misplaced. Women must refuse to atone on principle. It's not good for us, as individuals, or as a group.

Men, on the other hand, have much to atone for. As does society. By 'society' I mean patriarchy. I mean the destructive ideology that has taken hold of men and that gives rise to so much needless suffering for women and girls. I mean the contempt for the female that causes us all to devalue women and to be unmoved by their situation. I mean the pernicious doctrines of motherhood that put all the responsibility for children on women – and all the blame.

It's time for a feminist reversal of the patriarchal reversal. Let's get out the flip chart:

Men who were absent, addicted, or indolent while their children were growing up, who were not present to share the work and responsibility of raising their children, need to atone.

Men who abuse the mother of their children need to atone.

Men who use children as pawns to control their mother need to atone.

Men who plunge women into fear by threatening to take their children need to atone.

Men who rape, batter, control and neglect the mothers of their children, then have the audacity to fight to the death to wrest their children from them, claiming before the courts that the women are mentally unwell and unfit mothers, top my list of those who need to atone.

Men who violate women in systems of pornography and prostitution need to atone.

Men who fail to care for and honour women on their maternal journeys, particularly when they are pregnant or struggling in the role of mother, need to atone.

Men whose selfish actions or omissions may have contributed to the state of mind of a child who dies by suicide need to atone.

At the societal level, all institutions must atone for failing to keep women at the centre of laws, policies and practices. Due to our reproductive role, women are required to give so much more than men. Gestating, bearing and nurturing children makes us vulnerable in so many ways. Why are our institutions not doing everything in their power to protect and support women as mothers?

The justice system, particularly, needs to atone for its appalling dereliction of duty when it comes to mothers. Mothers need first and foremost to be safe. The best interests of the child will be served in a society where their mothers are safe and supported. The well-being of the mother must be central in determining custody and access. Keeping children with their mother must become the default position of the courts.

A woman must be allowed to cut ties completely with any man who abuses her, regardless of whether he is her children's father.

Mothers must not be separated from their children.

There are countless societal factors brought to bear on children's lives, aside from the family environment. A misogynist, racist, homophobic, capitalistic, warring culture can in no way provide the conditions in which children will flourish. When a child does not make it, the community as a whole needs to shoulder the burden.

Patriarchy's coup de grâce is manipulating mothers into thinking they are responsible for the suicide of their child. And for this, it must atone.

Bibliography

Abdallah, Asmaa and Nadeen Shaker. (Spring 2018). 'My principle is to unveil the mind'. *Cairo Review of Global Affairs*. <https://www. thecairoreview.com/q-a/my-principle-is-to-unveil-the-mind/>.

Benjamin, Marina. (12 August 2023). 'George Orwell's Unacknowledged Debt to His Wife Eileen'. *The Spectator*. <https://www.spectator.co.uk/ article/george-orwells-unacknowledged-debt-to-his-wife-eileen/>.

Brown, Laura S. (1994). *Subversive Dialogues: Theory in Feminist Therapy*. New York: Basic Books.

Bryan, Patricia L. (1997). 'Stories in Fiction and in Fact: Susan Glaspell's "A Jury of Her Peers" and the 1901 Murder Trial of Margaret Hossack'. *Stanford Law Review,* Vol. 49, No. 6, pp. 1293–1363.

CBC Radio. (9 May 2024). 'Why your teen might think rough sex is the norm'. <https://www.cbc.ca/listen/live-radio/1-63-the-current/ clip/16064829-why-teen-might-think-rough-sex-norm>.

Chesler, Phyllis. (1972/2005). *Women and Madness.* Chicago: Chicago Review Press. Fully revised and updated 2005 Edition by Palgrave Macmillan.

Chesler, Phyllis. (1986/1991). *Mothers on Trial: The Battle for Children and Custody.* New York: McGraw-Hill; San Diego: Harcourt Brace Jovanovich.

CTV News. (20 September 2021). 'Detective who solved murder of Ontario doctor says killer made big mistake trying to hide his crime'. <https://toronto.ctvnews.ca/detective-who-solved-murder-

of-ontario-doctor-says-killer-made-big-mistake-trying-to-hide-his-crime-1.5591745>.

Cunliffe, Emma. (2011). *Murder, Medicine and Motherhood.* Oxford: Hart Publishing.

Dalton, Nia. (14 December 2023). 'Emotional diary entries by mum Kathleen Folbigg cleared of murdering four babies after 20 years'. *Mirror*. <https://www.mirror.co.uk/news/world-news/emotional-diary-entries-mum-cleared-31672676>.

de Beauvoir, Simone. (1949/2009). *The Second Sex.* Translated by Constance Borde and Sheila Malovany-Chevallier. New York: Random House/Alfred A. Knopf.

Dickens, Charles. (1843). *A Christmas Carol.* London: Chapman & Hall.

Eger, Edith. (2020). *The Gift.* New York: Scribner.

Frankl, Viktor E. (1985). *Man's Search for Meaning.* New York: Washington Square Press.

Funder, Anna. (2023). *Wifedom: Mrs Orwell's Invisible Life.* New York: Alfred A. Knopf.

Gerster, Jane. (19 April 2019). 'Elana Fric was killed after filing for divorce. How do we make leaving less dangerous?' *Global News.* <https://globalnews.ca/news/5172976/domestic-violence-and-divorce/>.

Glaspell, Susan. (1927). *A Jury of Her Peers.* London: Ernest Benn.

Government of Manitoba. (Retrieved 22 February 2024). 'The Impact of Domestic Violence on Children'. <https://gov.mb.ca/justice/vs/dvs/impact.html>.

Gowriluck, Caitlyn. (12 February, 2024). 'Manitoba man charged with 1st-degree murder in deaths of partner, 3 children and partner's relative'. *CBC News.* <https://www.cbc.ca/news/canada/manitoba/carman-deaths-shock-manitoba-1.7112473>.

Hitchiner, Reverend Sally. (9 October 2022). 'Bloom where you're planted'. Sermon preached at St. Martin-in-the-Fields, London.

Jaffe, Peter G. and Claire V. Crooks. (February 2005). 'Understanding Women's Experiences Parenting in the Context of Domestic Violence: Implications for Community and Court-Related Service Providers'. *Violence Against Women Online Resources.* <https://familyserviceregina.com/wp-content/uploads/2016/05/parentingindv.pdf>.

Johnson, Donna F. (2012). 'Creating a Space for Mothers Who Have Lost a Child to Suicide'. In Gina Wong (Ed.). *Moms Gone Mad: Motherhood and Madness, Oppression and Resistance.* Ontario, Canada: Demeter Press.

Johnson, Donna F. (13 December 2022). 'Society prefers dead women to women who fight back'. *4W.* <https://4w.pub/society-prefers-dead-women/>.

Lerner, Gerda. (1986). *The Creation of Patriarchy.* Oxford and New York: Oxford University Press.

Levine, Helen and Alma Estable. (1981). 'The Power Politics of Motherhood: A Feminist Critique of Theory and Practice'. Occasional Paper. Ottawa: Center for Social Welfare Studies, Carleton University.

Li, Meng. (17 October 2022). 'Guilt and compensation: The interplay between maternal emotions and parent–child relationships in migrant families'. *Family Relations: Interdisciplinary Journal of Applied Family Science,* pp. 1607–1624.

Lundrigan, Samantha, Ruth Weir, Andrew Newton, Kelly Agudelo and Mandeep Dhami. (2022). 'Patterns and Predictors of Stranger Rape Locations'. *European Journal on Criminal Policy and Research,* Vol. 30, pp.181–209. <https://doi.org/10.1007/s10610-022-09535-5>.

Martin, Fern and Catherine Younger-Lewis. (1997). 'More than meets the eye: Recognizing and responding to spousal abuse'. *Canadian Medical Association Journal,* Vol. 157, pp. 1555–1558.

McClung, Nellie L. (1915). *In Times Like These.* Toronto: McLeod and Allen.

McDermott, Quentin. (28 April, 2019). 'Kathleen Folbigg to give her version of what diary entries about her dead children meant'. *ABC News.* <https://www.abc.net.au/news/2019-04-28/kathleen-folbigg-to-speak-to-inquiry-about-diary-entries/11051128>.

McDonald, Catherine. (13 February 2024). '"They should be named": Ontario family speaks after mother, baby murdered in home'. *Global News.* <https://globalnews.ca/news/10292667/mother-baby-murdered-richmond-hill-home-identified/>.

MacKinnon, Catharine A. (2007). *Are Women Human? And Other International Dialogues.* Cambridge Massachusetts: Belknap Press.

Mom's Choice Awards. (11 February 2023). '18 Moms Describe What It Means to be a Mother.' <https://www.momschoiceawards.com/?s=18+Moms+Describe+What+It+Means+to+be+a+Mother>.

Moran, Rachel. (2013/2015). *Paid For: My Journey Though Prostitution.* North Melbourne: Spinifex Press; New York: W. W. Norton and Company.

Morris, Steven. (20 October 2021). 'Woman stabs husband and tells police "I admit it all," footage shows'. *The Guardian.* <https://www.theguardian.com/uk-news/2021/oct/19/woman-stabs-husband-tells-police-admit-all-footage-shows-penelope-jackson>.

Mundie, Jessica. (19 April 2023). '"Keira's Law" passes Senate, signalling a change to the way courts approach domestic violence'. *CBC News.* <https://www.cbc.ca/news/politics/keira-kagan-domestic-violence-coercive-control-1.6815711>.

Rich, Adrienne. (1976). *Of Woman Born: Motherhood as Experience and Institution.* New York: W. W. Norton.

Rich, Adrienne. (1979). *On Lies, Secrets, and Silence: Selected Prose 1966-1978.* New York: W. W. Norton.

Rich, Adrienne. (1983). *Sources.* Woodside: The Heyeck Press.

Ritchie, Hannah. (8 June 2023). 'Kathleen Folbigg: Misogyny helped jail her, science freed her'. *BBC News.* <https://www.bbc.com/news/world-australia-65830799>.

Roper, Caitlin. (2022). *Sex Dolls, Robots and Woman Hating: The Case for Resistance.* Mission Beach: Spinifex Press.

Shakespeare, William. (1890). *Measure for Measure.* London: Cassell and Company.

Takševa, Tatjana. (2017). 'Mother Love, Maternal Ambivalence, and the Possibility of Empowered Mothering'. *Hypatia*, Vol. 32, No. 1, pp. 152–168.

Toews, Miriam. (2018). *Women Talking.* Toronto: Knopf Canada.

United Nations Office on Drugs and Crime. (2021). *Killings of women and girls by their intimate partner or other family members.* <https://www.unodc.org/documents/data-and-analysis/statistics/crime/UN_BriefFem_251121.pdf>.

Wells, Jamelle. (22 February 2023). 'Kathleen Folbigg diary entries not an admission of guilt, inquiry hears'. *ABC News.* <https://www.abc.net.au/news/2023-02-22/kathleen-folbigg-diaries-not-guilt-admission-inquiry-told/102008358>.

Whitbourn, Michaela. (22 February 2023). 'Folbigg diaries do not contain "true confessions of guilt," inquiry told'. *The Sydney Morning Herald.* <https://www.smh.com.au/national/nsw/folbigg-diaries-do-not-contain-true-expressions-of-guilt-inquiry-told-20230222-p5cmgc.html>.

Woolf, Virginia. (1929). *A Room of One's Own.* London: Hogarth Press.

Index

Other books in the Spinifex Shorts Series

Born Still: A Memoir of Grief
Janet Fraser

How did we move so far from love that a mother's grief becames the vehicle with which to punish her?

Losing a baby during childbirth is one of the most heartbreaking things imaginable. But to then be accused of causing that death is nothing short of soul-destroying. Janet Fraser's story shows what happens when private grief is turned into a public accusation against a woman who dared to exercise choice about how and where she gave birth.

This sobering book demonstrates the penalties dished out to women who question medical orthodoxy and to make decisions for themselves about their own bodies.

When things go wrong in a hospital, it is seen as unavoidable, and no one is to blame, as the medical institutions are seen as the arbiters of decision-making. The layers of bureaucracy protect insiders. Yet if a baby dies in a home birth, the full weight of the law comes down upon the woman who dared to give birth outside a hospital.

Janet Fraser is that woman and this is her story of injustice, loss and grief. This painful yet enlightening book shows that the patriarchy still wrestles for the control of women and their bodies – and punishes them with every tool in the legal handbook when they contest the view that their bodies are public property.

ISBN 9781925950120   ebook available

Surrogacy: A Human Rights Violation
Renate Klein

Pared down to cold hard facts, surrogacy is the commissioning/buying/ renting of a woman into whose womb an embryo is inserted and who thus becomes a 'breeder' for a third party.

Surrogacy is heavily promoted by the stagnating IVF industry which seeks new markets for women over 40, and gay men who believe they have a 'right' to their own children and 'family foundation'. Pro-surrogacy groups in rich countries such as Australia and Western Europe lobby for the shift to commercial surrogacy. Their capitalist neo-liberal argument is that a well-regulated fertility industry would avoid the exploitative practices of poor countries.

Renate Klein details her objections to surrogacy by examining the short- and long-term harms done to the so-called surrogate mothers, egg providers and the female partner in a heterosexual commissioning couple. Klein also looks at the rights of children and compares surrogacy to (forced) adoption practices.

It is the global advertising campaigns that groom infertile couples and gay men that have led to the establishment of multibillion cross-border industries: money made literally from women's flesh.

ISBN 9781925581034   ebook available

In Defence of Separatism
Susan Hawthorne

An examination of the controversy around women's spaces.

When a political group wants to strategise so that its members can arrive at agreed-on political tactics and ideas, they call for, and create, separate spaces. These might be in coffee shops, in community centres, in one another's homes or in semi-public spaces such as workers clubs, even cinemas. When the proletariat was rebelling, they did not ask the capitalists and aristocracy to join them (even if a few did); when the civil rights movement started it was not thanks to the ideas and politics of white people (even though some whites joined to support the cause); when the women's liberation movement sprang into life, it was women joining together to fight against their oppression.

The difference is that women are supposed to love men.

Through careful argument, Susan Hawthorne takes us through the ideas which are central to her case. She analyses the nature of power, oppression, domination and institutions and applies these to heterosexuality, rape and romantic love. She concludes with a call for women, all women no matter their sexuality, to have separate spaces so they can work together to change the world and end patriarchy.

ISBN 9781925950045   ebook available

Detransition: Beyond Before and After
Max Robinson

I experienced my transition as a form of resistance, but in reality it only affirmed the same stereotypes that had done me harm to begin with. Trying to prevent myself from committing suicide by becoming less recognizably female was an attempt at resistance that, politically, functioned in many ways as a form of capitulation.

Many feminists are concerned about the way transgender ideology naturalizes patriarchal views of sex stereotypes, and how that ideology encourages transition as a way of attempting to escape misogyny.

In this brave and thoughtful book, Max Robinson goes beyond the 'before' and 'after' of the transition she underwent and takes us through the processes that led her, first, to transition – in an attempt to get relief from her distress – and then to detransition as she discovered feminist thought and community.

The author makes a case for a world in which all medical interventions for the purpose of assimilation are open to criticism. Robinson's bold discussion of both transition and detransition is meant to provoke a much-needed conversation about who benefits from transgender medicine and who has to bear the hidden cost of these interventions.

Transition is not an unconstrained choice when we are fast-tracked to medical intervention as if being female was a tumor that required immediate removal to save our lives.

ISBN 9781925950403   ebook available

Transgender Body Politics
Heather Brunskell-Evans

Transgenderism in the twenty-first century is patriarchy emblazoned in imperial form.

Philosopher and activist Heather Brunskell-Evans shows how, in plain view under the guise of liberalism a regressive men's rights movement is posing a massive threat to the human rights of women and children everywhere. The transgender agenda has redefined diversity and inclusion utilising the language of victimhood.

In a complete reversal of feminist gender critical analyses, sex and gender are also redefined: identity is now called 'innate' (a 'feeling' located somewhere in the body) and biological sex is said to be socially constructed (and hence changeable). This ensures a lifetime of drug dependency for transitioners, thereby delivering vast profits for Big Pharma in a capitalist dream.

This eye-opening book does not shirk from the challenge of meeting the politics of liberalism and transgender rights head on. Everyone who cares about the future of women's and children's rights must read it.

The micro-politics and the macro-politics of identity interact to form one of the most misogynistic expressions of patriarchy in recent times under the guise of equality, diversity and inclusion.

ISBN 9781925950229   ebook available

From the 'Neutral' Body to the Posthuman Cyborg: A Critique of Gender Ideology

Silvia Guerini

If the human being is allowed to be genetically manipulated and made by artificial means in the laboratory in an unstoppable crescendo of experimentation, what will be left to defend?

This book is a radical critique of gender ideology and transhuman design. Silvia Guerini shows how the TQ+ rights agenda is being pushed by eugenicist capitalist technocrats at the top of Big Business, Big Philanthropy, Big Tech and Big Pharma companies. She explains how fundamental struggles such as the fight against genetic engineering and the fight against artificial reproduction can only advance in conjunction with an opposition to gender ideology. By linking 'gender identity' to the genetic modification of bodies, she warns that humanity itself is at risk of becoming a synthetic life form with synthetic emotions within a virtual, fluid, deconstructed metaverse.

Today, being revolutionary means preserving everything that makes us human. It means defending the living world and nature as entities to be respected, not as parts that can be broken down and redesigned in a laboratory world.

The idea of the 'neutral' body and body modification pave the way for the construction of the post-human cyborg and the genetic engineering of bodies. Is the last bioethical barrier about to be breached to give way to transhumanist demands? And at what cost?

ISBN 9781925950885   ebook available

Bibliodiversity: A Manifesto for Independent Publishing

Susan Hawthorne

In a globalised world, megacorp publishing is all about numbers, about sameness, about following a formula based on the latest megasuccess. Each book is expected to pay for itself and all the externalities of publishing such as offices and CEO salaries. It means that books which take off slowly but have long lives, the books that change social norms, are less likely to be published.

Independent publishers are seeking another way. A way of engagement with society and methods that reflect something important about the locale or the niche they inhabit. Independent and small publishers are like rare plants that pop up among the larger growth but add something different, perhaps they feed the soil, bring colour or scent into the world.

Bibliodiversity is a term invented by Chilean publishers in the 1990s as a way of envisioning a different kind of publishing. In this manifesto, Susan Hawthorne provides a scathing critique of the global publishing industry set against a visionary proposal for organic publishing. She looks at free speech and fair speech, at the environmental costs of mainstream publishing and at the promises and challenges of the move to digital.

ISBN 9781742199306   ebook available

*If you would like to know more about
Spinifex Press, write to us for a free catalogue, visit our
website or email us for further information
on how to subscribe to our monthly newsletter.*

Spinifex Press
PO Box 105
Mission Beach QLD 4852
Australia

www.spinifexpress.com.au
women@spinifexpress.com.au